Empty Your Bags. Unlock Your Potential.

Trekking Through Life's Terrains, Overcoming Challenges And Achieving Newer Heights

Ajay Rawat

Ukiyoto Publishing

All global publishing rights are held by

Ukiyoto Publishing

Published in 2023

Content Copyright © Ajay Rawat

ISBN 9789360166830

All rights reserved.
No part of this publication may be reproduced, transmitted, or stored in a retrieval system, in any form by any means, electronic, mechanical, photocopying, recording or otherwise, without the prior permission of the publisher.

The moral rights of the author have been asserted.

This book is sold subject to the condition that it shall not by way of trade or otherwise, be lent, resold, hired out or otherwise circulated, without the publisher's prior consent, in any form of binding or cover other than that in which it is published.

www.ukiyoto.com

Dedicated to both my parents,
who continue to inspire me

Carry six empty bags
for success in
the journey of life

|| अहं ब्रह्मास्मि ||

"Aham Brahmasmi" is a Sanskrit phrase that translates to "I am Brahm" or "I am the ultimate reality." Brahm is a term used in Hinduism to refer to the ultimate reality or the divine essence that underlies the universe.

Preface

"Empty Your Bags. Unlock Your Potential" is a book that stands out in the self-help genre because it's not just another "how-to" book promising quick fixes to all your problems. Unlike most books in this genre, it's not written by someone trying to sell you their coaching services or promote their group and practices. Instead, it's a compilation of the best practices followed by the world's best coaches and training organizations. The core essence contains some of common principles taught by world's best coaches minus any religious connect. I am the author of this book but more than that I am a fellow seeker who has been on the same journey as you readers and I am sharing valuable experience along the way.

As the author, I started my journey with a simple goal of improving my time management. However, as I began attending more and more training sessions, I realized that other aspects of my life needed improvement, including my relationships, health, and finances. It was during one of these training sessions that I had a breakthrough moment and realized that I needed to let go of the baggage I had been carrying and embrace new perspectives and ways of thinking. This realization set me on a path of self-discovery that eventually led me to write this book.

"Empty Your Bags. Unlock Your Potential" is divided into eight chapters, each focusing on a different aspect of personal growth and development. In the second chapter, I encourage readers to empty their bags of mind let go of the clutter in their thoughts, and to focus on their goals and dreams. This sets the tone for the rest of the book, where I provide practical advice and tools for readers to unlock their full potential.

The third chapter delves into the importance of unlearning and relearning new skills, which is essential for personal and professional growth. In this chapter, I explore the patterns that hold us back and how to break free from them. This is followed by an in-depth discussion of various mind models and how they can help readers understand their motivations and desires.

In the fourth chapter, I focus on the importance of leveraging our time, which is a finite resource that we must use wisely. In the fifth chapter, I emphasize the importance of authenticity in inspiring others to join us on our journey. Chapter six examines the habits and behaviors that can either help or hinder us on our path to success and provides practical tips for creating structures that support our goals. Finally, in chapter seven, I encourage you readers to dream again, armed with the knowledge and tools necessary to achieve their goals.

What makes this book unique is that it's a condensed version of the best practices followed by the world's best coaches and training organizations. It's not just a rehash of common self-help advice. Rather, it's a culmination of my personal experience and research, distilled into practical advice that readers can apply to their own lives.

As a fellow seeker, I wrote this book as a set of notes from someone who has been on the same journey as the readers. I believe that personal growth and development are ongoing processes, and there's always room for improvement. Whether you're a seasoned self-help enthusiast or just starting on your journey, "Empty Your Bags. Unlock Your Potential" provides a fresh perspective and practical advice that will help you achieve your dreams and unlock your true potential.

Index

1. **The departure**

   Embrace a mindset of simplicity by leaving behind the world of accumulation. Discover the transformative power of simplification, where it all begins with a dream and the courage to pursue it.

2. **Empty your bag of mind** – Dream and focus

   Dream, decide and simplify your life by asking, "Why carry more in life for your happiness and well-being?" Achieving great things is possible with minimizing resources and focusing on maximizing efficiency, creativity, and strategic thinking.

3. **Empty your bag of knowledge** – Rethink and unlearn

   Unlearn and learn new skills effectively by emptying your knowledge bag and limitations about what you can do. Recognize what's filling up your mind space, understand brain patterns and human behaviour models for optimized learning and prioritize growth.

4. **Empty your bag of time** – Leverage and expand

   Dream big and forge new relationships and teams to achieve goals that are beyond one's optimum capacity. Reimagine and accomplish what's possible in finite time. Build and nurture relationships to unlock new opportunities.

5. **Empty your bag of heart** – Inspire and involve

   Expand your impact by connecting with more people in your big ambitious dreams. Authenticity and purity of heart are the secret ingredients to inspire to involve them. Make genuine and long-lasting relationships.

6. **Empty your bag of habits** – Break patterns and collaborate

   Gain insights into your patterns and formation of habits that derail you from your goals, leading to repetitive situations. Construct supportive structures to overcome these habitual hinderances, paving the way for success and achieving new results.

7. **Empty your bag of know-hows** – Reset and restart

   Be cautious of falling the trap of feeling accomplished when learning new tools and methods. Instead, recognize the importance of resetting and starting fresh on new journeys to foster ongoing growth and exploration.

8. **Arrival**

   In the journey of life, you have the freedom to choose what and how much to pack. Trust in the universe's support as you embark on this adventure. Remember, you have arrived at this moment, ready to embrace the path ahead.

Contents

Introduction	1
The Departure	7
Empty Your Bag Of Mind	35
Empty Your Bag Of Knowledge	51
Empty Your Bag Of Time	119
Empty Your Bag Of Heart	149
Empty Your Bag Of Habits	193
Empty Your Bag Of Know-Hows	235
Arrival	271
Glossary	291
Acknowledgement	309
About the Author	*317*

Introduction

Whether you are interested in self-improvement books or a new reader with curiosity. You've probably attempted quick solutions to make your life better. However, resulting momentary successes might leave you feeling deflated when you find yourself back in the same situation.

There's no dearth of resources promising to help you achieve your goals, but how many of them actually deliver long-lasting results? If you're looking for something unique that will keep you on the path to success, then this book can help. Whether you've attempted self-improvement programs before or are just getting started, this book can help you reach your true potential. So, are you ready to take the next step in your life? Let's get started. You will definitely find something new and worthwhile, no matter why you chose this book. This book contains concepts that have been around for centuries, yet they still apply and are practical. Taking advantage of these will bring you success in any area of your life.

My Creative Director experience, along with training, books, videos, and coaching, has provided me the knowledge needed to excel in my career and other aspects of my life. This book offers practical advice and resources for individuals wishing to broaden their horizons and realise their potential. These concepts can help you in achieving greater heights, enabling you to dream bigger and achieve more in any aspect of your life. If you're a professional looking to advance in your career, an

Empty Your Bags. Unlock Your Potential.

entrepreneur looking to develop a successful firm, or a person looking for a satisfying life, this book will offer you with the insights you need to get started. Through the pages of this book, you will learn the key principles that have enabled me to succeed in my career and personal life. You will discover how to develop a winning mindset, cultivate creativity, and harness the power of innovation. You will also learn the importance of effective communication, strategic thinking, and teamwork. Moreover, you will explore the transformative effects of passion, perseverance, and a growth mindset. With each chapter, you will gain new insights and practical strategies that you can apply to your life immediately.

The idea for this book came to me during a week-long high-altitude trek. I was completely disconnected from my busy life and without a phone or internet. Immersed in nature, I realized how valuable the lessons I learned on this trek were, and how they could be applied to life's journey. Therefore, I have used my trek's common theme and story to convey these valuable learnings to my readers.

You might be wondering why you should read the words of someone who's just an "average Joe" like me. Well, that's exactly who I am. I don't have a fancy degree from an Ivy League school or come from a famous family with lots of money. But I would love to share my insights and experiences with you that I gathered from numerous trainings for professional and personal development.

I've invested in a lot of different training sessions covering topics like health, finance, tech, bliss, satisfaction, meditation, writing, and living life to the fullest. I'm glad that I've grown because of all the work I've done and I'm delighted to share my insights. It's been a privilege to coach people as a volunteer and see them grow.

Despite my limited capacity, I've been able to make a positive impact on the lives of those I've coached. Recently, I invested around $5,000 in training from some of the world's best trainers. Thanks to advances in technology, I was able to take up multiple trainings in short time without giving up or compromising my work and family responsibilities.

I know paying for all those trainings is not and expenditure but is an investment. I believe it's important to stay up-to-date and relevant in an ever-changing world. It's also crucial to continually improve oneself to remain competitive in the industry and better serve clients and colleagues with your best possible version.

In this book, I've condensed all the valuable lessons and best practices I've learned through my training and personal experiences. My intention is to share these insights with you so that you can benefit and move forward in life with greater speed, feeling lighter and free.

My aim is to equip you with practical tools and guidance that go beyond surface-level changes, working on a deeper level of heart, mind, and habits. These strategies will help you overcome any obstacles and achieve success in all areas of your life.

Through this book, I provide you with a comprehensive approach to personal growth and development. By following the strategies outlined, you will be able to create positive changes in your life that will have a lasting impact. You will learn how to develop healthy habits, improve your mindset, and cultivate a positive outlook on life.

With this knowledge, you will be empowered to overcome any challenges that come your way and create a brighter future for yourself. By putting these strategies into practice, you can achieve success in all areas of your life, including relationships, career, health, and personal fulfillment.

My goal with this book is to inspire and empower you to take responsibility for your own journey as I share my experiences and insights with you. Everyone can achieve greatness and find fulfillment, but it requires dedication, hard work, and a willingness to learn and grow.

So, if you're looking for a fresh, no-nonsense approach to self-improvement, I urge you to give this book a chance. I may not have all the answers, but I promise to share with you what I've learned on my own journey. I will also inspire you to take action towards your own goals and dreams.

I invite you to join me on this journey of self-discovery and transformation, and I look forward to learning from you as well. Let us embark on this adventure together and see where it takes us.

In the process you might uncover the essence of true power, we must examine human behavior and personal experiences. Challenging conventional wisdom, we will look at various mind models for our actions and behavior. Instead, we will explore the possibility that there is something beyond our physical and emotional needs that drives us forward. In this lesson, we'll examine the idea that our decisions are based on our innermost values, beliefs, and principles. We can gain insight into our own motivations and behavior by delving into our understanding of the world.

This book is not only about exploring the epitome of power but also an invitation to re-examine what we carry with us on our journey through life. We often refer to life as a journey, which raises the question of what is truly necessary to bring with us and how much we should carry. The answers to these questions are not straightforward and may vary from person to person, but through this book, we aim to start a conversation and encourage self-reflection. This journey together will help unlock the secrets of the human mind and push the limits of what we believe is possible. Whether you are seeking personal growth, inspiration, or simply looking to broaden your horizons, this book is the perfect starting point.

This book has a couple of powerful tools, each tool has the ability to take your potential to an exponential level. If you start applying even a single tool the results are going to be amazing and you can practice them over time to master them. When used in combination, you can get results that you would have never imagined.

They give us ways to rethink our approaches, using available resources in a more effective way. Instead of quick wins, they provide sustainable approaches that challenge the typical mindset and encourage creativity and exploration.

I have given some exercises after specific chapters with those tools, to ensure that you get time in between to practice those tools. Once you practice them and make them part of your routine or use(consider) them while making decision, will provide great value and give you power and control in life without arrogance.

If you can master these tools then you become unstoppable and achieve next levels of success in your respective areas, be it business, finance, health, relationship, or contribution.

Ajay Rawat

The Departure

Leaving the world of accumulation.
Getting to know the power of simplification

Empty Your Bags. Unlock Your Potential.

As humans, traveling is an inherent part of our existence. We embark on journeys to explore, seek, and to expand our horizons. The dictionary defines a journey as moving from one place to another. But a journey or travel is much more than just moving from point A to point B. In fact, many people often describe life as a journey.

As we travel through life, we carry both tangible and intangible baggage that shapes our experiences. This leads us to ponder: How much should we carry to reach our desired destination?

This book is a testament to my pursuit of self-improvement and reaching new heights. I've collected invaluable lessons and remarkable discoveries along my journey, which continue to fuel my pursuit of growth and fulfillment. My aim in sharing these stories is to inspire you to discover your hidden potential. And ignite your passion for exploring new territories.

I vividly recall a moment of immense pride when I felt the weight of my achievement. Standing atop a summit in the Jammu and Kashmir region, near the India-POK border, I held my beloved Indian tricolor flag for the very first time. The summit towered at a staggering height of 4,000 meters. From there, I gazed upon the breath-taking beauty of the Gurez Valley. It felt surreal, considering that a mere three days prior, I had been leading a sedentary lifestyle as a couch potato in the comfort of my home in New Delhi.

Those were the days when I worked remotely because of the global pandemic caused by the Corona Virus.

The world was grappling with its impact, with many losing loved ones and others facing long-term medical conditions. Despite living in isolation, I contracted the virus not once, but twice. This took a toll on my physical health and compounded the difficulties I faced in my personal life. The medications and necessary dietary changes for y health resulted in a significant weight gain of 15 kilograms. The lack of physical activity, long working hours on my laptop, and binge-watching web series contributed to this unwanted weight gain. It didn't bother me much until my clothes refused to fit in.

It was 16th August 2021 when I stood atop that summit, holding our tricolor flag along with fellow trekkers. I realized the power of a dream and decision, irrespective of one's starting point.

We continued our high-altitude trek toward the captivating Patalwan Lake. It had crystal-clear water, mirroring the passing clouds and there was a gentle, cool breeze blowing. We traversed awe-inspiring landscapes that justified this land's well-deserved title of "heaven on earth." These experiences and the visuals imprinted in my mind shall forever remain cherished.

At the conclusion of our trek, we gathered for a cozy and relaxing get-together with the other 25 trekkers. Who are from diverse backgrounds and spanning ages ranging from 11 to 55 years. Our group leader presented each of us with certificates adorned with thoughtful citations. On my turn, the group leader recounted how I had started as one of the slowest members during the first two days of our trek. Yet something within me transformed, and I emerged as one of the fastest in the second phase of the trek.

To be honest, the significance of this change hadn't fully dawned on me until those carefully articulated words struck a chord. They made me reflect on what I had achieved and the person I had become during our trek. A transformation had taken place. This book encapsulates those moments and the life lessons I gleaned from the trek and other training experiences.

These experiences and lessons are the genesis of this book. The book explores life lessons I learned during the trek that have transformed the way I think, feel, and behave. These lessons give me transformed results in various aspects of my life, including health, finance, relationships, and my creative profession.

So, I invite you to join me on this incredible journey. Prepare yourself by putting on your backpack and lacing up your boots. Together, we will embark on an unforgettable experience.

Ajay Rawat

The moment of truth

I encountered this moment of truth during my high-altitude trek in the stunning Gurez valley of Jammu and Kashmir. Our goal was to push beyond the 4,000-meter mark on the third day, and all I had with me was my camera gear bag. As we trudged forward, my body grew weary, and I reached a point where I couldn't walk any longer. It was the moment that I realized I had to let go of my beloved camera bag. My camera holds great sentimental value to me.

It wasn't an easy decision to make. My camera gear was my lifeline; I had been carrying it everywhere with me, all the time. My camera bag had a whole lot of equipment. Camera bodies, different lenses—wide and telephoto—batteries, action cameras, and more. It was my connection with the world, a source of inspiration, and passion for me. But I was in no state to carry it anymore. I had to look for help.

Fortunately, I was able to find some local help in the form of porters who agreed to carry my camera bag. They had bags from other members of the group who were also struggling. The relief was palpable as I handed over my bag, knowing that it was in safe hands. It was a moment of liberation, and I felt like a weight had been lifted off my shoulders.

But it was more than just a physical burden that had been lifted. As I continued on the trek without my camera gear, I began to realize the importance of letting go and being open to new experiences. I had been so focused on capturing the perfect shot that I had forgotten to enjoy the journey itself. Without my camera gear, I became more present in the moment. I could appreciate the beauty around me at a different level. I could talk to other members of the trek more freely. I could sense some new kind of connection. Everything looked more beautiful somehow. And it was all because I had let go of my attachment to my camera gear.

When it was time to head back to our base camp, a 3-4-hour trek away, I was filled with energy and a new sense of purpose. I led the pack, or at least, that's what it felt like. With the weight of my camera gear gone, I felt lighter, more agile, and more connected to the environment around me. It was a transformative experience, and one that I will never forget.

Looking back at my trek, I realize that my experience was not just about the physical journey. It was also a journey of the mind and soul. I learned the importance of letting go and being open to new experiences. I realized that sometimes in the pursuit of our dreams and aspirations, we become so focused on accumulating material goods and possessions that we forget to live in the present and enjoy the journey. But when we let go of our attachments, we open ourselves to new possibilities and experiences that we may have never imagined.

Ajay Rawat

I came to understand that our attachments, whether physical or emotional, can hold us back from reaching our destination.

We live in a modern society where we are constantly being told that we need more of the newest products, the latest technology, and other commodities to be happy and fulfilled. We are continually reminded through messages, visuals, advertising, media reports, and other outlets that display what is deemed as the optimal standard of beauty, wealth, intelligence, success, love, and happiness.

The story does not end there . Social media magnifies the pressure to fit in and appear successful. Where we are encouraged to share every aspect of our lives with others. We feel the need to show off our material possessions, travels, and relationships as if these things define our worth. We want to prove to our friends, family, and even strangers on the internet that we are living a good life and are successful. This pressure to maintain an image can be overwhelming. It can lead to feelings of inadequacy and stress. It's essential to remember that our self-worth and happiness should not be tied to material possessions or what others think of us.

The material possessions we acquire in life do bring us happiness and satisfaction, but it is often short-lived. We tend to feel content with our possessions until we see someone else with something bigger, better, or fancier than what we have. This can be a neighbor with a larger house, a friend with a fancier car, a colleague with a higher job title, or someone with more money in their account.

Our desire to belong often stems from the social norms and expectations that are ingrained in us since childhood. As we grow up, we start to compare ourselves with others in our social circle and strive to match their lifestyle and possessions to fit in. The pressure to conform to the societal norms of success, beauty, and wealth often leads us to accumulate material things, which we hope will bring us happiness and a sense of belonging.

However, this pursuit of materialistic desires often leads to a constant need for more, as we compare ourselves to those who have more than us. We get trapped in a cycle of wanting more and never feeling satisfied with what we have, leading to a feeling of emptiness and unhappiness.

The concept of the hedonic treadmill describes this phenomenon, where we are constantly chasing happiness through materialistic possessions, yet we are never truly happy as we adapt to our new possessions and desire even more.

It's not just about the external factors that contribute to our dissatisfaction, but also about our internal mindset. Even if we achieve our goals and acquire material possessions that we once longed for, we may still feel a sense of emptiness or lack of fulfillment. I would like to use the term 'disenchantment' here.

Material possessions appear to be the ultimate goal of our lives. Then why do we often experience a sudden or gradual disenchantment in achieving life's purpose?

We might experience disenchantment with what we have acquired after a long struggle and hard work. Even if these are external factors such as material possessions, fame, or success. Perhaps the initial satisfaction and happiness that came with the acquisition faded away over time. Leaving a sense of emptiness.

As humans, we tend to adapt to our circumstances. What was once exciting and novel becomes the new norm. We may start to take it for granted. We may begin to focus on what we don't have rather than what we do have. It can lead to feelings of disappointment and dissatisfaction. It's a trap that can be difficult to escape from, as we may feel like we need to keep acquiring more to feel happy and fulfilled.

So, are these material possessions a source of happiness and satisfaction? if yes, then why they are so short-lived? There seems to be something wrong with this picture. We believe that by accumulating more, we can achieve our dreams and reach our goals. But in reality, this constant pursuit of material goods only adds to our stress and burdens us with more responsibilities and obligations. We end up spending more money, making more arrangements, and adding more and more to our already full plate. This can lead to a never-ending cycle of wanting more, which can cause us to feel overwhelmed and dissatisfied with our lives.

Could it be possible that true happiness and fulfillment are not where we keep looking for them, in external factors and material goods? Are we relying too much on external factors?

External factors like our boss to give us a raise, for our clients to sign a deal, win that award, or buy something that we have been aspiring to in the show window for a long time?

If that is the case then why did Muhammad Ali, one of the greatest boxers of all time, throw his Olympic gold medal into the Ohio River in 1960? A gold medal, which he got after years of training, and practice. As they call it blood, sweat, and tears.

Why Robin Williams, one of Hollywood's most celebrated comedy actors, took his own life in 2014, despite the love and support he received from his family, friends, and fans regardless of his success or popularity?

Why did Chuck Feeney, who co-founded Duty-Free Shopper, and was a billionaire, decide to give away almost 8 billion USD, most of it anonymously? And what's more, why does he say that he's never been happier in his life? Finally, why does Chuck Feeney advocate for the idea of giving while living?

Why did Prince Charles and Lady Diana break up after a fairy tale love story? That was the most high-profile marriage coming to an end with all the controversies along with it.

Why did Jeff Bezos, the founder of Amazon divorce his wife MacKenzie Scott after 25 years of marriage? This divorce resulted in one of the largest settlements in history, with Scott receiving billions of dollars in assets.

Why did this sudden or gradual disenchantment with things appear as the whole purpose of life? Why do they start looking so meaningless?

Is the answer within us?

I have realized that true happiness and fulfilment come from within. And it's essential to cultivate a sense of inner peace and contentment. This realization has given me a newfound appreciation for the simple things in life and the importance of letting go of my attachments to material goods. I want to carry this newfound wisdom forward into my plans and dreams, ensuring that I don't get caught in the trap of material accumulation. Instead, I want to focus on creating meaningful experiences, forming deep connections with others, and pursuing my passions with purpose and joy.

The trek I embarked on was one of the most exhilarating experiences of my life. As I hiked through the challenging terrain, I realized that this journey was only made possible because I had taken on something new and different, something outside of my comfort zone. It was the goal that I had set for myself, the dream that I aspired towards, that kept me going. This realization made me appreciate the power of dreams and the role they play in shaping our actions.

Ajay Rawat

It all starts with a dream

Our dreams are the fuel that drives us forward. They are the aspirations we hold for ourselves and the vision we have for our lives. Whether it's a desire to travel the world, start a business, learn a new skill, or pursue a career, our dreams serve as a compass, guiding us towards our desired destination. Without a dream or a goal to aspire towards, we can easily fall into a state of stagnation, lacking the motivation to push ourselves to achieve more.

The importance of having a dream or a goal cannot be overstated It provides a sense of purpose and direction, something to strive for and work towards. When we have a clear vision of where we want to go, we can make better decisions and take the necessary steps. Even if we encounter obstacles or setbacks, our dreams give us the resilience and determination to keep going. Without this sense of purpose, we can feel lost and directionless, unsure of what steps to take. That is like a dried fallen leaf drifting in the wind.

Of course, dreams come in many different forms, shapes, and sizes. Some people dream of achieving financial success and accumulating wealth, and some dream of making a positive impact on the world. Some people dream of finding love and starting a family, and some dream of traveling the world and experiencing different cultures. The beauty of dreams is that they are unique to each individual—reflecting our own desires, values, and aspirations. No dream is too big or too small, as long as it has meaning and purpose for the individual pursuing it.

Dreams are the defining brushstrokes that set humans apart from the rest of the animal world. Contemplating the power of dreams unravels a profound differentiator between the human and animal experience. A unique ability that transcends survival and delves into the art of living. This essence draws a stark line, where animals navigate the world driven solely by instinctual needs to survive, and humans, with their evolved brains, possess an extraordinary ability not just to survive but to truly live.

At its core, the power to dream becomes a beacon guiding humanity beyond the mere act of survival. Animals, driven by primal instincts, find their existence confined to favorable ecological pockets, adapting to the immediate necessities of food, water, and shelter. Their lives are a perpetual cycle of instinctual responses to the environment, a survival dance choreographed by nature's rhythm.

In contrast, the human race, armed with the profound gift of dreaming, steps beyond the boundaries of survival. Dreams become the catalyst for exploration, discovery, and creation. They ignite the human spirit, propelling individuals to venture into inhospitable terrains and conquer daunting challenges. The power to dream is, in essence, the power to live beyond surviving.

Dreams, in their purest form, are the blueprints of a life lived not in reaction to the environment but in response to the aspirations that dwell deep within the human soul.

Dreams elevate existence from a series of reactions to a deliberate and intentional journey of exploration and creation. In the realm of dreams, the ordinary transforms into the extraordinary, and the mundane becomes the canvas upon which masterpieces are painted.

Dreams are the bridge between surviving and thriving, between existing and truly living.

As humans, we are wired to dream and aspire for more. From a young age, we are encouraged to dream big and aim high. We are taught that success equals wealth and that we should strive to accumulate as much money as possible. We envision ourselves living in big houses, driving fancy cars, and having a fat bank account, as these are the social symbols of success. However, have we ever stopped to question whether this is the only path to achieving our dreams? Have we considered the individuals who have made a difference in the world, and the impact they have had on others?

Success is not solely defined by material possessions or financial prosperity. Many of the world's most accomplished individuals have made a difference through their contribution to society, then accumulating wealth. They have left a lasting impact on the world, and their legacy lives on through the lives they touched. These individuals are a testament to the fact that success is not just about financial success but about making a meaningful impact on others.

On the other hand, some people have found happiness and fulfillment in leading a life of simplicity and minimalism. By choosing to live with less, they have been able to focus on what truly matters in life—relationships, experiences, and personal growth. They have found joy in the simple things, such as spending time with loved ones, traveling to new places, and pursuing their passions. By adopting a lifestyle that aligns with their values and priorities, they have been able to achieve the kind of contentment and satisfaction that material possessions cannot provide.

The dreams we have and the goals we set for ourselves can shape our actions and ultimately determine the trajectory of our lives. It is important to take the time to reflect on what we truly want out of life, and what our definition of success looks like. Is it about accumulating wealth and material possessions, or is it about making a difference in the world and finding personal fulfillment?

The pursuit of materialistic dreams has been the norm in our society for a long time. It is not uncommon for individuals to aspire towards materialistic possessions such as fancy cars, big houses, and designer clothes. There is nothing wrong with having material goals, it is important to recognize that they are often a means to achieve something else that is non-physical or intangible.

Many people mistakenly believe that the acquisition of material goods will bring them happiness and fulfillment. However, studies have shown that once our basic needs such as food, shelter, and clothing are met, the correlation between material wealth and happiness begins to diminish. This is because material possessions are temporary and fleeting and they do not provide lasting satisfaction. On the other hand, experiences and relationships can provide long-term happiness and fulfillment.

We discussed a few paragraphs before how our conditioned view of society, norms, and peer pressure compels us to acquire more material goods that are considered symbols of success, so why bother chasing our so-called dream and aspirations?

Dreams aren't really the same as real goals. However, they are still important because they help us decide what we want in life. We pick our goals based on what we think success looks like. Even if our happiness from achieving these goals doesn't last very long, they still give us a sense of satisfaction.

Our goals and dreams can also tell us what we really want in life. Sometimes it's hard to know what we want, but our dreams can help us figure it out. These desires are often tied to our values.

We all have noticed that our dreams can change as we grow and learn. What we wanted in the past might not matter to us anymore. And achieving our goals doesn't guarantee long-term happiness. True happiness comes from within us, not from what we have or achieve.

That is why I emphasise recognizing that our material dreams are often a means to achieve something else. For example, one might dream of owning a large house, but the underlying motivation could be to provide a comfortable home for their family. Or one might dream of owning a fancy car, but the underlying motive could be to feel successful or accomplished. In these cases, it is important to question whether material possession is truly necessary to achieve the underlying motive or if there are other ways to achieve the same result.

On the other hand, some dreams may center around making a positive impact on others or the world at large. These dreams are often altruistic and reflect a sense of purpose beyond personal gain. By channeling our energies towards achieving such dreams, we can leave a lasting legacy that benefits society as a whole. It is important to recognize that such dreams may not necessarily bring us materialistic gains, but they can give us a sense of fulfillment and purpose that can transcend material possessions.

By understanding the nature of our dreams and the underlying motivations, we can make conscious choices that align with our values and beliefs.

I invite you to explore the deeper motives behind our material dreams using the "Five Whys" or "Three Whys." These principles are used for problem-solving and identifying the root cause. However, I find them remarkably effective in deciphering my aspirations for material possessions. This introspective process helps unveil the true objectives I aim to achieve.

By comprehending the motives behind our dreams, we gain the ability to make conscious choices aligned with our values. Whether we are inclined towards materialistic pursuits or aim to generate a positive impact, a thoughtful examination of our dreams guarantees genuine satisfaction and fulfillment. This fusion of minimalist principles and the probing "Whys" acts as a compass, urging us to pursue simplicity and authenticity in our journey toward realizing our dreams.

Empty Your Bags. Unlock Your Potential.

Ajay Rawat

Succeed with minimalism

In the age of consumerism and materialism, the younger generation has started to move towards a minimalist lifestyle. They are seeking to live a life of purpose and significance, which is free from the clutter and distractions of modern society.

Minimalism is a worldview that emphasizes the significance of living with less and focusing on the basics, not only tidying or possessing fewer stuff. The goal is to eliminate unneeded distractions and make room for what actually matters.

One advantage of living a minimalist lifestyle is that it allows for more focus and clarity. With less distractions in our environment, our minds can focus on what is genuinely important. We may eliminate the distractions and noise that keep us from achieving our goals and objectives. Instead, we might devote more energy and drive to our hobbies and goals. This can assist us in achieving our objectives more swiftly and efficiently.

Minimalism is not a new concept. Minimalism is a timeless concept that has been embraced and exemplified by numerous individuals throughout history, emphasizing the power of simplicity and essentialism. An exceptional illustration of this philosophy can be found in the life and work of Steve Jobs, a renowned figure and co-founder of Apple Inc. Jobs' unwavering commitment to minimalism not only echoes the core principles of this ideology but also showcases its remarkable effectiveness in various domains.

Steve Jobs, a visionary and innovator, understood that true elegance and functionality lie in simplicity. He firmly believed that by stripping away the unnecessary and focusing solely on the essentials, one could achieve extraordinary results. This minimalist approach to design permeated every aspect of his work, leading to the creation of revolutionary products that would transform entire industries and shape the course of technological advancement.

The iPhone, one of the most iconic devices of our time, is a testament to Jobs' commitment to minimalism. By reimagining the smartphone, he eliminated the complexities and clutter that plagued traditional mobile devices. Jobs' relentless pursuit of simplicity resulted in a sleek, streamlined design that allowed users to effortlessly navigate through a multitude of functions, making technology more accessible and intuitive for the masses.

Similarly, the iPad, another ground-breaking creation, embodies the principles of minimalism in its purest form. Jobs' vision for the iPad was to provide a portable and versatile computing device that would remove the need for multiple gadgets. By consolidating various functions into a single, minimalist tablet, he eliminated the superfluous and empowered individuals to work, create, and consume media with unparalleled convenience and elegance.

Steve Jobs' commitment to minimalism went beyond just the physical design of products; it extended to how consumers experienced those products and even how they were marketed. Apple, under Jobs' leadership, prioritized simplicity and minimalism in every aspect.

Apple not only strived to design products with clean and straightforward interfaces, but they also recognized the necessity of offering a consistent user experience. Jobs thought that by removing extraneous complications, users would be able to focus on what was truly important—the enjoyment and functionality of the device itself.

Apple's marketing campaign was modest, in keeping with their minimalist philosophy. Rather than overwhelming customers with technical specifics, Apple chooses to focus on the benefits and entire experience of its products. They believed that rather than overloading users with technical details, they should allow them to make informed decisions based on the value and quality of the product.

Despite their minimalistic marketing approach, Apple remained dedicated to producing best-in-class products. Year after year, with each new release, Apple consistently set new industry benchmarks by pushing the boundaries of innovation and performance. Their commitment to excellence remained unwavering, even as they maintained a minimalist approach to marketing.

The success of Apple's minimalist design philosophy not only propelled the company to new heights but also inspired a wave of minimalistic design trends across diverse sectors, including fashion, architecture, and interior design.

However, minimalism extends far beyond the pursuit of success or the creation of innovative products. It encompasses the profound desire to live a life imbued with meaning and purpose, one that resonates with our deeply-held values and beliefs. It prompts us to shift our focus from material possessions to the aspects of life that hold true significance – our relationships, experiences, and personal growth.

When we embrace minimalism, we embark on a journey of self-discovery and introspection. By intentionally reducing the clutter in our lives, both physical and mental, we create space to appreciate and cherish the things that truly enrich our existence.

Through the practice of minimalism, we gain a fresh perspective on our priorities. We are empowered to critically examine the choices we make, ensuring that they align harmoniously with our core values.

As we let go of the ordinary, we discover newfound freedom. We free ourselves from the burdensome weight of excess belongings, commitments, and expectations. In this liberation, we find the space for the extraordinary.

Furthermore, accumulating material possessions and wealth does not always lead to happiness or fulfilment. In fact, research has shown that beyond a certain level of income, extra money does not bring more happiness. Instead, it is our relationships and experiences that bring us the most joy and fulfilment. By embracing minimalism, we can shift our focus towards the things that truly matter and find greater happiness and fulfilment in our lives.

"I think everybody should get rich and famous and do everything they ever dreamed of, so they can see that it's not the answer."

-Jim Carry

In this famous quote, Jim Carrey expresses his perspective on wealth and fame, suggesting that while it may be tempting to desire riches and popularity, they do not necessarily bring true happiness or fulfillment.

Carrey's statement reflects his belief that material wealth and fame alone do not guarantee a meaningful and satisfying life. He implies that individuals should have the opportunity to pursue their dreams and achieve financial success, but they should also recognize that true contentment lies beyond material possessions and external validation.

As people get older, they tend to lose interest in having lots of things because they have already experienced and seen many of them. They realize that there are more important things in life. On the other hand, the younger generation has grown up in a time of plenty and didn't have to struggle for resources like previous generations did. Because of this, they have a different perspective on things.

In recent years, many young people have started embracing minimalism. They want their lives to be more meaningful and freer from the distractions of our busy society. Simplifying their lives helps them focus better and have a clearer sense of what they want to achieve. They are also more aware of the environmental damage caused by excessive consumption.

Minimalism isn't just about owning fewer things. It's a way of thinking that focuses on living with less and focusing on what really matters. Many successful and influential people, like Steve Jobs, have practiced minimalism throughout history. By embracing minimalism, we can learn to appreciate the important things in life and find greater happiness and fulfillment.

Let's take Mahatma Gandhi as an example. He was a very important person in the 1900s, but he chose to live a simple and minimalistic life. He believed that by living this way, he could understand and help ordinary people better. Gandhi fought for fairness and equal rights. He inspired millions of people worldwide and played a significant role in India gaining its independence. Even though Gandhi passed away over 70 years ago, there are still many people today who follow his lifestyle and beliefs.

The minimalist lifestyle is not just limited to historical figures and famous individuals. We spoke about growing trend among young people today, who are embracing minimalism. They view it as a way to live a more fulfilling life. By reducing their possessions and focusing on the essentials, they are better able to align with their values and pursue their passions.

People who wear designer labels and drive flashy cars are no longer considered successful. According to study, such materialistic goals frequently indicate insecurities and a "not good enough" mentality. People are waking up to the fact that showy material possessions do not always guarantee happiness or fulfillment.

We cannot underestimate the power of simplification. Reducing distractions and focusing on what truly matters, can help us achieve our ambitious goals and make a lasting impact on the world. Whether you are a 30-something-year-old looking to live a more meaningful life or an entrepreneur seeking to make a difference, the principles of minimalism and simplification can help you achieve your dreams. So why not give it a try and see the difference it makes in your life.

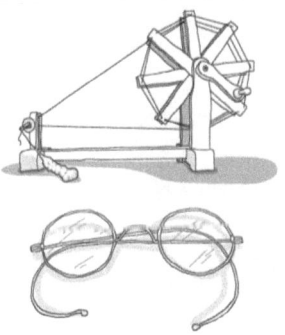

Empty Your Bags. Unlock Your Potential.

Ajay Rawat

Empty Your Bag Of Mind

Dreams and decisions

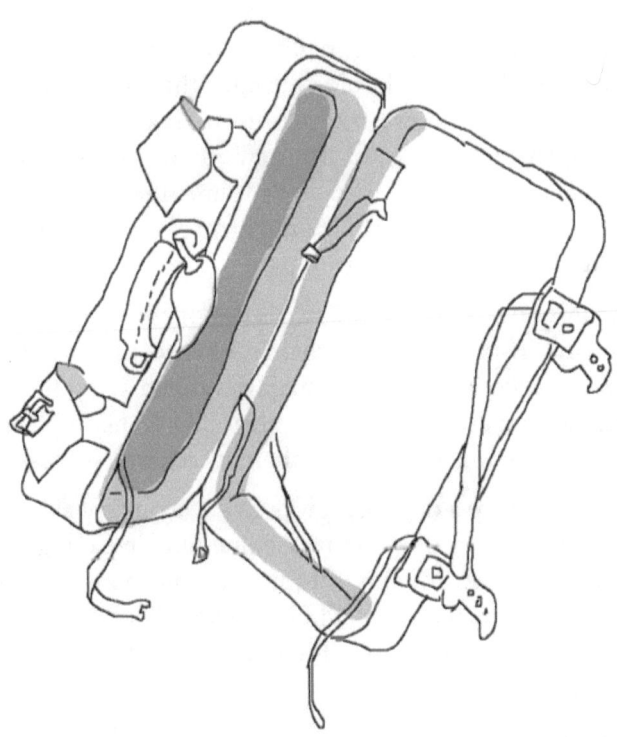

Empty Your Bags. Unlock Your Potential.

Dreams are a powerful force that can change our lives. We already learned about their importance in the previous chapter. Dreams give us a sense of purpose and light up our path. They go beyond our current situation and show us what we want for the future. But dreams alone stay in our imagination unless we have the courage to make decisions. Decisions turn our dreams into real accomplishments. They need us to be brave, determined, and willing to take risks. Making decisions can be scary because we might doubt ourselves or feel uncertain. But we shouldn't forget the potential we have inside. When we take action and make decisions, we open ourselves up to new opportunities and amazing experiences. So, let's remember what we learned before and embrace the power of decisions to make our dreams come true.

Dreams and decisions are two sides of the same coin. Dreams inspire us and provide a sense of purpose, while decisions offer a roadmap towards making those dreams a reality. Without one, the other is incomplete, and it's essential to combine them to achieve success.

When we have a dream, it gives us a reason to wake up each day and strive towards something meaningful. Dreams can be anything, from traveling the world to starting a business or finding love. They give us direction and help us stay focused on what we want in life.

Decisions are the practical steps that bring our dreams to life. Making decisions requires us to take responsibility for our actions and commit to making our dreams a reality. It can be challenging to take that first step, but it's necessary to turn our dreams into something tangible.

The journey towards our dreams can be daunting, and it often requires us to step outside our comfort zones. We need to be ready to face our fears and take risks. But the rewards that come from pursuing our dreams are worth it. The journey may have ups and downs, but the satisfaction that comes from achieving our goals is immeasurable.

Making decisions towards our dreams is the first step to transformation. It teaches us to switch from being reactive to be proactive and take charge of our lives. This leads to increased self-confidence and independence, and it opens up new opportunities that were previously out of reach or imagination.

It's important to remember that dreams and decisions are not stagnant. Our dreams may change over time, and the decisions we make towards them may change as well. It's important to be open to adaptation and to keep moving forward towards our goals.

And remember, the journey from dreams to decisions is not always easy, but it is always worth it.

The COVID-19 pandemic and the resulting lockdowns had a huge impact on the lives of people around the world. I remember those days vividly. Along with medical challenges, the pandemic brought a lot of fear and uncertainties. We all tried to navigate this new and unknown threat. There was news from around the world about people getting sick and dying due to COVID-19. Unfortunately, some of us even lost our loved ones to the virus.

As the situation got worse, governments around the world-imposed lockdowns and restrictions to try and curb the spread of the virus. These restrictions meant that we were confined to our homes, with limited opportunities to step out except for essential activities like buying groceries or seeking medical attention. These lockdowns had a significant impact on our daily lives. We suddenly found ourselves cut off from our usual routines, with no access to schools, offices, gyms, restaurants, or movie theatres.

Despite the difficulties, people adapted to the circumstance in their own unique ways. Many of us discovered new ways to pass the time, such as watching movies and TV series on the internet or experimenting in the kitchen with new dishes. We have found ways to stay in touch with family and friends by using video chat apps.

I was no exception. The lockdown meant a significant change in my daily routine as well. I was used to going to work every day but suddenly found myself working from home. This presented a new set of challenges. I struggled to maintain a work-life balance while being confined to my apartment. At first, it felt nice to wear casual clothes while working from the comfort of home and not worry about the daily commute. But soon enough, the monotony of working from home started to set in.

During this time, I also tried to learn new skills and hobbies to pass the time. I started taking online cooking classes and even tried my hand at gardening. These activities provided a welcome distraction from the anxiety and uncertainty of the pandemic.

One day, one of my close friends called me to join him on a high-altitude trek to a valley that I never heard of. The destination had only recently opened to tourism, making our group the first to explore the area. This prospect was a stark contrast to my usual lifestyle of being a couch potato.

The trek was set to take place above 4000 meters, which was a daunting prospect in itself. We would have to forgo the usual amenities like proper accommodation, kitchen, electricity, and most importantly, phone and internet connectivity. These things had become crutches during the prolonged lockdown period we had all experienced. The idea of leaving them behind was both exhilarating and nerve-wracking.

There were some safety concerns in the region, as this place is quite close to border area. It was a whole new world that I would be stepping into, and I would be meeting many new people for the first time. Despite these uncertainties, I was eager to seize the opportunity and experience something completely out of my comfort zone.

Empty Your Bags. Unlock Your Potential.

Honestly, at first, I was hesitant. The idea of embarking on a journey into the unknown was daunting, and I worried that I wasn't up to the physical and mental challenges that lay ahead. But the more I thought about it, the more I realized that this was exactly what I needed. I needed to push past my limits, to explore new horizons, and to find meaning and purpose in my life.

I started researching the trek, pouring over maps and guidebooks, and reaching out to others who had done it before. I invested in gear and supplies and started training my body and mind for the journey ahead. Each day brought new challenges, but also a sense of purpose and excitement that had been missing from my life for far too long.

As the day of the trek approached, I felt a mix of excitement and nerves. I was ready to embark on this adventure, but also acutely aware of the risks and uncertainties that lay ahead. But I knew that this was a journey I had to take, for myself and for my own growth and fulfillment.

Looking back on those pre-journey experiences and thoughts, I realize now how much they shaped me and prepared me for what lay ahead. The decision to go on that trek was one of the most important ones I have ever made, and it opened up a world of possibilities and experiences that I never could have imagined.

Ajay Rawat

Act to decide

As someone who has spent a lot of time on the couch, I found myself in a predicament. I had been leading a sedentary lifestyle for far too long and knew that I needed to change it. I wanted to challenge myself and step out of my comfort zone, so I decided to go on a trek.

For me, the difference between a wish and a decision was clear. A wish is passive and lacks action. It's a hope that something will happen. There is no real expectation of taking action to make it happen. It's like wishing for rain where we have no control over the weather. Our wish is unlikely to make any changes. Wishing is a form of helplessness, as we place our hopes in external factors rather than taking control of our own lives.

On the other hand, a decision is an active choice that involves taking action towards a goal. It requires a bold approach, a willingness to change to achieve the desired outcome. When we make a decision, we take responsibility for our lives and take action to create the change we want to see. We are willing to make big or small changes to ourselves and our surroundings, in order to achieve our goal.

Making decisions is an essential aspect of human life. We make so many small and big decisions in our lives. In fact, you might get surprised to know that an adult human being makes 35000 conscious decisions every day.

However, it's not enough to make a decision without setting a time-bound target. The statement "A decision without a time-bound target is a glorified wish" implies that any decision made without a specific deadline is merely an aspiration rather than a commitment. The significance of setting a timeline when making decisions is important as it provides focus, direction, and accountability to the decision-making process.

When there is no clear timeframe in place, a decision lacks urgency, and this can be an easy target for procrastination. Procrastination is the tendency to delay or postpone an action, and it's a habit that can be detrimental to decision-making. With no specific deadline or timeline, it's easy for individuals to push back the decision, telling themselves they will do it later. That results in a failure to act on their intentions.

Procrastination can cause significant damage to the decision-making process. The more time that passes without any action, the more the decision loses its momentum, and the likelihood of success dwindles. The lack of progress can lead to frustration and loss of confidence, and ultimately, the decision may not be implemented at all.

When we do not set a specific timeline for our decisions, we might end up spending too much time contemplating the decision rather than taking action. While it is essential to consider different perspectives and weigh the pros and cons of a decision, delaying action can lead to analysis paralysis. It make us stuck in indecision.

Moreover, without a timeline, it's challenging to track progress and measure success. That impacts our accountability. Accountability is crucial in decision-making, as it helps individuals to take responsibility for their actions and hold themselves accountable for the outcomes.

Deciding to go on a trek was a big step for me. I knew that it would require a lot of effort, planning and preparation. But I was determined to follow through on my decision and make it a reality. I started by researching the trek and figuring out the best route to take. I also began to focus on my physical fitness, taking steps to improve my stamina and endurance.

As I started to plan and prepare for my trek, I began to see the benefits of making a decision. I was learning new skills and gaining valuable experience that would serve me well in other areas of my life. I was becoming more confident and self-assured, and I knew that even if my first attempt was not successful, I would learn from my mistakes and try again.

In deciding to go on a trek, I also had to accept that there would be risks involved. There was apprehension of something going wrong. but I was willing to take that risk in order to challenge myself and grow as a person. Making a decision requires courage. The willingness to face uncertainty can get us tremendous rewards.

Empty Your Bags. Unlock Your Potential.

As I embarked on my trek, I felt a sense of accomplishment and pride. I had made a decision and followed through on it, and the experience had taught me so much about myself and my capabilities. It was a stark contrast to my former couch potato lifestyle, and I knew that I had made the right decision in taking on this challenge.

As I had mentioned earlier, I put a lot of effort into preparing for my trip. It included buying the necessary items, selecting appropriate baggage, and planning the transportation of my belongings from a plane to a cab and up to the mountain camp. I also had to plan how much to carry from the base camp to the destination point on the peak.

I accumulated more and more. Buy more, plan more, carry more, and worry more.

The tendency to accumulate more and more possessions and belongings is a common phenomenon in today's world. We buy more, plan more, and carry more, thinking that we are better prepared for any situation that may arise. However, in reality, this excessive accumulation often leads to unnecessary weight and inconvenience, making our journeys more difficult than they need to be.

Our dreams and decisions are intricately connected, and achieving our aspirations often requires a shift in our mindset. As we strive to reach our goals, we may become fixated on accumulating more possessions, planning more activities, and taking on more responsibilities. However, this mindset can lead us away from our true purpose and leave us feeling overwhelmed and unfulfilled. This is where a minimalistic mindset can be helpful.

By embracing a minimalist approach to life, we can simplify our lives and focus on what truly matters. This means letting go of the excess and focusing on the essentials. When we adopt a minimalistic mindset, we become more intentional in our decision-making. We focus on the things that truly bring us joy and meaning and let go of the rest.

In the pursuit of our dreams, a minimalistic mindset can help us make more thoughtful decisions. Which further aligns with our values and long-term goals. We learn to say no to commitments that do not serve us and to focus our time and energy on the things that matter most. By doing so, we can move closer to our dreams and find greater happiness and fulfillment along the way.

A minimalistic mindset can be a powerful tool in achieving our dreams. By simplifying our lives and focusing on what truly matters, we can make more intentional decisions that bring us closer to our goals. So, let us embrace the power of minimalism and pursue our dreams with intention and purpose.

During my trek, I learned the importance of letting go and being open to new experiences. I realized that sometimes in our pursuit of our dreams and aspirations, we become so focused on accumulating material goods and possessions that we forget to live in the present and enjoy the journey. But when we let go of our attachments, we open ourselves up to new possibilities and experiences that we may have never imagined. Photographers tend to do this a lot, including myself. At times we get so focused on taking pictures that we miss living the experience at that moment.

Being a creative professional, I fully recognize the significance of dreaming and decision-making in my career. In fact, the whole essence of creativity is to strike a balance between dreaming and deciding. We always have to assess when to stop dreaming and when to decide. Decide which idea to go with.

There is a creative exercise called Blue sky thinking, which involves exploring unconventional and imaginative ideas. It is a vital aspect of creative thinking and innovation. However, decision-making is equally crucial. As a creative director, I believe that the ability to make informed decisions is critical to achieving success.

In this book, I emphasize the importance of dreaming and deciding, which can aid individuals in unlocking their creativity and generating innovative solutions to problems. In the first chapter, "Empty Your Mind Bag" we explored how unburdening oneself of mental baggage can enhance creativity and innovation.

Through the practice of emptying my mind and making decisive choices, I have personally experienced the profound impact it can have in overcoming creative blocks and generating breakthrough results.

This approach not only led to personal satisfaction, but also to immediate success with my clients and audience.

My experience with emptying my mind and making decisive choices has convinced me of the universal applicability of these practices, not just in the context of creative work, but in all areas of life. The power of dreaming and deciding cultivates new ways of thinking and working that can lead to innovative solutions and breakthrough results in any field. Therefore, I encourage everyone to adopt these practices and tap into their full creative potential to unlock new possibilities and achieve greater success.

"It is in your moments of decision that your destiny is shaped."
-Tony Robbins

Is it really that important to **empty your Mind bag**—empty from how much to accumulate or what for?

Dreams, which are so potent and can alter the course of history. They are only conceivable if and only if your mind is clear of cares and anxieties and not occupied with gathering items that you believe are significant.

Making decisions involves emptying the mind bag of distractions and doubts.

Empty Your Bags. Unlock Your Potential.

Exercise:
List down your dreams you will like to accomplish in:

1 week:
_____
_____
_____

1 month:
_____
_____
_____

1 year:
_____
_____
_____

Long term dreams:
_____
_____
_____

List down your decisions to fulfil above listed dreams:

_____
_____
_____
_____
_____

Important exercise:
1. Celebrate if you have listed your dreams you are working towards
2. Celebrate if you have made decisions to fulfil your dreams.
3. Celebrate as and when you tick your listed dreams

Empty Your Bags. Unlock Your Potential.

Ajay Rawat

Empty Your Bag Of Knowledge

Develop

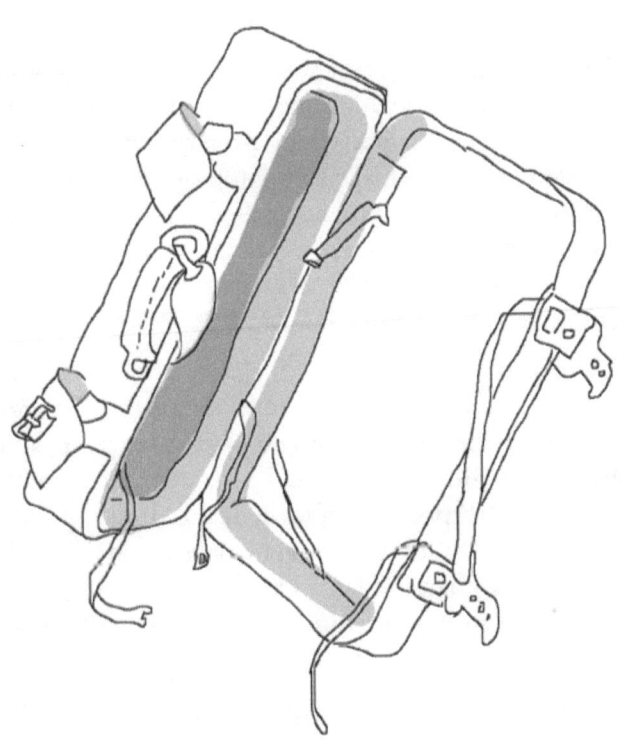

Empty Your Bags. Unlock Your Potential.

I made sure to have the suitable luggage by trying out different ruck sacks and back packs to see which would accommodate all my stuff. The rucksack I finally picked was big enough to fit all my essential items. I did a mock packing, and wow, it still had 1/4th of the space empty. It made me quite happy about my choice of bag. Surprisngly, on the night before my morning flight, I had to struggle to close my bag. I did not know how come the same big bag seems much smaller. Obviously, I packed many more items.

Now with such a large and heavy bag, my concerns also increased. Will it be within my check-in baggage limit? How will I transport everything from the airport to the base camp and eventually to the top of the mountain? Airport and base camp was still easy as there were proper transport arrangements, but what happens to the bags when we ascend towards the summit? How will I carry all that weight and climb 3000-4000 meters?

We reached the airport, the luggage weight was just about the limit, and we boarded the flight. We got down at the airport, took the cab to the base camp, and things were OK. However, as I began the ascent with my bulky backpack, I quickly realized that I had overpacked. The excess weight made the trek much more difficult than it should have been. In hindsight, I should have given more thought to what I was packing and prioritized the essentials.

Most people in the trekking group requested help with the bags, and we somehow managed to get some potters and mules to carry our stuff. Thank god, that made things far more easier.

The trek itself was really enjoyable, despite its challenges. I had a great time and couldn't help but think about going on another trek in the future. Next time, I wanted to go during winter because I imagined it would be even more fun with snow all around, and I hoped to capture some gorgeous pictures. However, at that moment, I became scared and worried about how much more I would need to pack for a winter trek. What if we didn't have the support of porters and mules next time? Would I be able to carry all my belongings on my own? These concerns bothered me multiple times throughout the trek.

Monks and gTum mo

Do you know about those Buddhist monks meditating on the top of snow-capped mountains with minimal clothing? These monks have mastered the art of mental and physical control through years of meditation and asceticism.

Extreme conditions on the mountain during winter makes it challenging to survive, still, these monks take it in their stride. They can stay focused and disciplined regardless of the weather or temperature. By developing the power to regulate their body temperature, they have been able to not only survive in harsh conditions but also use their own body heat to dry wet clothes on their bodies.

I was intrigued by this concept, and after some research, I got to know a little more detail about this practice by Tibetan Buddhist monks, which is called g-tum mo, or inner fire. It is a well-known practice among Tibetan Buddhist monks living in the remote Himalayan mountains. It involves a series of breathing exercises and visualization techniques that enable the practitioner to generate heat from within their own body, raising their core temperature and keeping themselves warm.

gTum mo is a Tibetan word, also spelled tumo, or Tum-mo; which has a Sanskrit translation to caṇḍālī or chandali. g Tum mo literally means 'fierce woman or goddess'. Tummo is also the Tibetan word for 'inner fire.'

The practice of gTum mo is often taught as part of the ancient Tibetan meditation system of Tummo. The goal of this practice is to develop a strong mind-body connection and increase overall awareness, ultimately leading to a greater sense of inner peace and well-being.

A group of scientists from Harvard and other universities studied three Tibetan Buddhist monks with this skill of gTum Mo Yoga. gTum Mo could generate heat from within their bodies. All this was inside test labs with very low temperatures. The researchers found that one of the monks raised the temperature of his fingers and toes by almost 15 degrees Fahrenheit in just a few minutes of meditation. The other two monks also showed significant increases in finger temperature. These monks have been practicing this skill for a long time by drying ice-cold, wet sheets draped over their bodies during chilly nights in the Himalayas.

The results amazed the researchers, which showed that the mind has a significant influence on the body's ability to fight the cold. Harvard scientists studied this interesting phenomenon of how the mind can affect the body's physiology. This skill allows the monks to carry less warm clothing when they travel, which can be an advantage in harsh environments.

It's true that everyone has different genetics or comes from diverse geographic or cultural backgrounds. However, even people who are different in these

Empty Your Bags. Unlock Your Potential.

aspects can learn and practice this technique of gtum mo, which allows them to raise their body temperature. It shows that this technique can be learned and developed with consistent practice.

I am wondering if having the capability of gTum Mo could be very useful to be able to pack lighter for a journey, allowing for fewer items of clothing and gear to be carried and thus making the journey smoother and more efficient.

Furthermore, g-tummo isn't only limited to Tibetan monks. Through regular practice and guidance from experienced teachers, anyone can learn to harness the power of their own inner fire and use it to improve their physical and mental well-being, even in extreme conditions.

These monks meditating on the mountain are a reminder to us all that we can learn to develop our inner abilities. The lesson here is that it is possible to live a fulfilling life without the need for excessive material possessions.

Ajay Rawat

Drinking water

I already told you that I had a big list of things to get before the trek. I put all the stuff in my backpack. This was the most planned trip I've ever been on, and I listened carefully to the experts leading our group. They told us to buy the right kind of shoes, different types of socks, upper coverings, appropriate lowers, caps, rain covers, binnies, trekking poles, miscellaneous items, and so on. However, they also suggested that we purchase LifeStraw bottles or oversized water bottles, but I did not buy them.

On the first day of the trek, I noticed many people were carrying large water bottles, and a few also had lifestraw bottles. I didn't feel like I needed them, so I didn't get them. I thought it would be okay to find water on the way, and I also had a steel mug with me, which I could use to drink water from streams. I felt prepared and confident with my choices and was ready to start the trek.

During the trek, I noticed that those who had bigger bottles or lifestraw bottles were constantly worried about the quality of water available in the mountains. They kept checking and filtering water repeatedly. They also ran out of water more frequently and would become upset, negatively impact their trekking experience.

In contrast, those of us with a steel mug could drink directly from the streams, which was convenient and saved us from worrying about running out of water. We felt confident and well-prepared. It was fun to drink water straight from the streams. We also enjoyed the feeling of being close to nature and not having to rely on too much equipment.

I noticed that carrying an extra 3-4 kilos of weight, mainly because of large water bottles, impacted people's ability to walk comfortably, especially at higher altitudes. Those with the extra weight had to rely on sticks and trekking poles for support, which was tiring and inconvenient. On the other hand, those who were confident in managing with fewer things had less baggage and could help others more effectively. They could lend their trekking poles to those in need, provide water, and offer moral support.

Being confident in using available resources can change our mindset and perspective, like drinking water from streams, making trekking poles from driftwood, and lighting a fire with twigs and dried leaves. Drinking directly from the streams was not only enjoyable but also allowed us to connect more closely with nature. It made us feel more connected to the environment and gave us a sense of independence and self-reliance.

Kids traveling international

Talking about my impromptu, no plans traveling nature, there is one more exception besides my Gurez Valley trek, where I made equally elaborate plans before travel. The second instance had all those things like clothes, shoes, luggage, medicines and pretty much everything, but it wasn't for me; it was for my 12-year-old daughter, who was going on a school exchange program to Russia for the first time.

As a parent, I naturally had concerns about her being in a foreign country for the first time without us. Especially one with a different language and culture. One of my biggest concerns was her food. I knew she wouldn't find Indian food there unless they went to a specific Indian restaurant. The likelihood of finding an Indian restaurant was very less outside Moscow, and these kids were also going to smaller cities in Russia. So, we decided to pack a lot of ready-to-cook or heat-n-eat food packets for her, enough for each day of her trip. I didn't want her to struggle without proper food, and I wanted her to have food of her choice and taste.

Looking back, I realize that we made all this effort because my daughter was too young and was in a foreign land without resources. But, what if an adult had to plan a trip in similar conditions?

Many, including myself, still carry ready-to-cook meals or pre-packaged food when traveling because we're unsure if we'll have access to a kitchen or the ability to cook our food.

Having the skill to prepare meals using locally available ingredients like vegetables, bread, and rice can be really useful, especially when visiting places with limited food options. It means we don't have to rely on local restaurants and waste time and money searching for suitable places to eat.

Being able to cook for ourselves is a valuable skill. Not just for survival but also for immersing ourselves in a new world. The local cuisine, understanding the culture, and connecting with the local people. It gives us a sense of self-sufficiency and opens up opportunities for richer experiences during our travels or in a situation where certain types of food are scarce.

It is natural to feel apprehensive when traveling to a new place with different language and culture. However, with the right skills, one can adapt and thrive in adverse conditions without carrying excess baggage. As seen in the examples discussed, acquiring new abilities such as cooking with available ingredients or using natural water sources can significantly reduce the need to carry extra food or water. This not only reduces the physical weight of the luggage but also relieves the mental burden of worrying about running out of supplies.

My daughter returned from her 10-day stay, and she told me that she had only used only one or two of the packets. So, all that effort of arranging, packing, and carrying them to Russia and back was in vain.

Traveling light has many benefits. It saves money and gives you the freedom. Freedom to explore new places without carrying heavy bags or running out of supplies. Therefore, it is always worth investing time and effort in learning new skills to manage and thrive in adverse conditions, whether it is for a short trip or an extended stay in a new place. With practice and experience, one can learn to adapt and enjoy the experience of travel with minimal luggage. It makes your journey much more comfortable and memorable.

Consider if somebody is going to inhuman or hazardous places? Should one carry their whole world with them?

Ajay Rawat

Survival reality shows

In recent times some survival-based TV shows have become increasingly popular. These shows feature individuals or groups attempting to survive in extreme environments, such as remote forests, deserts, or mountains, with limited resources and facing various challenges. Some popular examples include "Survivor," "Naked and Afraid," "Alone," and "Man vs. Wild."

One of the primary reasons for the popularity of these shows is the sense of adventure and excitement they provide. The uncertainty of the situation creates a sense of suspense and anticipation, keeping viewers hooked.

However, these shows also provide valuable insights into the basic necessities of human survival. They demonstrate that humans do not necessarily need the luxuries and conveniences to survive. Instead, they show that survival depends on fundamental needs such as shelter, water, food, and warmth.

'Man vs. Wild' is a popular TV show that originally aired on the Discovery Channel from 2006 to 2011. The show features British adventurer and survival expert Bear Grylls, who has a background in British Army special forces. He has skills such as climbing, sailing, and mountaineering. In the show, he was dropped from a helicopter without any food, water, or elaborate tools into remote and harsh terrains. Places like deserts, jungles, islands, and mountains. He has to use his survival skills such as hunting and gathering food, building shelters, starting fires, and navigating treacherous terrain using natural resources available to him to stay alive. The show was praised for its realistic portrayal of survival situations and for promoting a minimalist approach to survival. as he travels to some of the most inhospitable places on earth and demonstrates his skills at surviving in the wild.

One of the unique aspects of Man vs Wild is that Grylls often puts himself in very dangerous situations to demonstrate survival techniques. For example, he has climbed down waterfalls, jumped off cliffs, and swam through freezing rivers.

Through the show, Grylls emphasized the importance of understanding one's surroundings and being resourceful with what's available in nature. The show also highlighted how society's desires for luxury items and technology are not necessary for survival. Rather, basic survival skills and knowledge of the environment can go a long way in ensuring one's survival. Thus, Man vs Wild promoted a more minimalist approach to survival and encouraged viewers to rethink their need for excessive material possessions.

'Alone' is another popular survival TV show that premiered in 2015 on the History Channel. The show takes survival skill-based shows to a whole next level. It features ten contestants, common men, and women, left alone in a remote wilderness location, equipped with only minimal survival gear and cameras to document their experiences. The contestants are chosen based on their survival skills and experience, and challenged to survive as long as they can in the wilderness.

The contestants on Alone are dropped off in a remote location and are completely dependent on nature and the environment to create food, shelter, and safety. They are allowed to bring only a limited number of supplies, such as a knife, a bow and arrow, and a fishing net. They must forage for food, build shelter, and protect themselves from wild animals and harsh weather conditions. The show provides a unique insight into how humans can survive in the wilderness with minimal resources and how important it is to have survival skills and knowledge.

One of the main differences between Alone and other survival shows, such as Man Vs Wild, is the level of isolation. In Alone, the contestants are actually alone and must rely on their skills and resources to survive. There is no one to turn to for help or advice, and they must make all decisions themselves. It creates a sense of self-reliance and independence, which is not found in other shows. Additionally, the lack of a camera crew means that the footage is raw and unedited, giving viewers a more authentic look at what it takes to survive in the wilderness.

So, even a single person can survive with minimum or no resources and stay in inhabited places. Another testimony to the fact that people don't need much to survive, the rest are fancy wishes and desires.

Empty Your Bags. Unlock Your Potential.

'Naked and Afraid' is another reality TV show where two strangers are left in the wilderness for 21 days with no clothes, food, or water. The idea of the show is to see how humans would have survived in the past when they had to find food, water, shelter, and protection.

The contestants are regular people with no special survival training. They come from different backgrounds, like teachers, business executives, and construction workers. It makes the show relatable and inspiring to the viewers. The contestants have to build their shelter, find food and water, and protect themselves from danger. They face extreme weather conditions, predators, and limited resources. They have to work together and use each other's strengths to survive.

The contestants on Naked and Afraid don't wear any clothes, just like people did in prehistoric times. Which adds to the challenge and shows how vulnerable people can be.

The show illustrates that people don't need a lot of possessions to survive. Rather, the contestants develop new abilities and learn new skills to survive in the wild, strengthening them both physically and mentally. Which I am sure help them in their lives to achieve newer heights with satisfaction and fulfilment.

Ajay Rawat

Teach a man to fish

"Give a man a fish, and you feed him for a day; teach a man to fish, and you feed him for a life" is a powerful message about the importance of developing skills in our journey of life. It's a metaphor that can apply to different aspects of our lives, including packing for a trip.

When it comes to packing for a trip, the saying suggests that instead of carrying excessive baggage or relying on pre-packaged food, we should learn some basic skills necessary to cook and manage with available resources. It means that we should improvise with the ingredients and equipment we have at our disposal, instead of always relying on pre-packaged items. This way, we can travel light and be more self-sufficient, making our trip more enjoyable and fulfilling.

Similarly, in life, it is essential to develop the skills and abilities necessary to overcome challenges and succeed in our endeavors. This means that we should always be willing to learn and grow, not simply rely on our existing knowledge or abilities. By developing new skills and abilities, we become more adaptable and resilient, which enables us to navigate life's challenges with greater ease and confidence.

Relying on others for everything can be comforting, but it comes with its own set of limitations. When we depend on someone else to provide us with what we need, we become vulnerable and susceptible to their decisions. We may not have control over the situation and may not always get what we need. This is especially true when we're traveling to unfamiliar places where we may not have access to our usual sources of comfort. In such cases, learning how to cook or manage with the resources available to us is essential.

Similarly, in life, when we don't develop the skills necessary to navigate life's challenges, we limit ourselves and become dependent on others. But when we take the initiative to learn and acquire new skills, we become self-sufficient and empowered to create our own opportunities. We learn to overcome obstacles and succeed in our endeavors, making us more resilient and confident.

Developing new skills can be challenging, but it's a valuable investment in ourselves. It enables us to adapt to changing circumstances and overcome challenges, making us more independent and better equipped to navigate the journey of life. So, instead of relying on others for everything, we should embrace the power of learning new skills and take charge of our lives.

Another episode that emphasizes emptying the knowledge bag is to do with my preparation again but in a different way.

Ajay Rawat

Randomness in Cognitive Selection

I am about to embark on my trek to Gurez valley, a place I have never been before. While my ancestral roots lie in the Himalayas, I have never visited this particular set of mountains. I agreed to go on the trek with my friend and other group members, and have already paid for the trip and purchased most of the gear I need. I have also done some conditioning exercises to prepare myself for the high-altitude trek, which will take me up to 4000 meters above sea level.

One day, I decided to do some research on the place to get an idea of what it looks like and plan my camera gear accordingly. I searched for videos on the internet, but there weren't many available. It wasn't a very popular destination, which was one of the reasons I was excited to go on the trek in the first place. Eventually, I came across a few amateurish videos made by local people and travel guides.

From the videos, I could see that the place was beautiful and not very crowded, which was a good thing. The weather looked pleasant and not as cold as I initially thought, though still colder than Delhi or any other hill stations. I also saw a bunch of people going on a day trip from the valley, carrying some food and tea with them. It seemed like a nice short trip, and the video ended soon after.

However, I could also tell from the videos that the climb was going to be quite steep. Local people were seen walking with the help of sticks and taking breaks in between to catch their breath. This made me a bit apprehensive, but also excited for the challenge.

As I prepared for the trek, I couldn't help but feel a sense of anticipation mixed with a little bit of nervousness. I had never been to this place before, and I had no idea what to expect. But that was also part of the adventure. I had agreed to go on this trek precisely because it was an unusual destination, and I wanted to explore something new.

The day before Independence Day, I flew to Srinagar to begin our Gurez valley journey. The Indian Army guarded the airport and surrounding areas. After a wait, we set off for Gurez valley. The journey was a pleasant one, and we traveled in an SUV for three to four hours on nice roads. We took breaks for tea and meals, and the scenery kept getting more beautiful. The people were kind and hospitable. The hills were lush green, and the sky was blue. I had never seen such a magnificent view while crossing the pass. I enjoyed the company of my fellow travelers.

We discovered a simple cluster of houses at our destination. I wasn't sure if we could call it a town. Along a river with transparent water, houses were on both sides. The majestic mountain Habba-Khatoon was visible in the background. The base camp was by the river. I saw all these enthusiastic people of different age groups and introduced myself to a few. We set up our tent and admired the setting sun. We went for an acclimatization walk with our backpacks. The walk by the river was relatively flat. Day zero was easy.

The plan for the next morning was to ascend to a place called Disson. I recognized the name because I had seen a video of this picnic spot during my research. I knew a little bit about how the place looked like, how people were climbing, and how steep the climb was.

The next morning, we all gathered after a light breakfast, and with the help of the Indian army and local authorities, we set off for the climb with some nice celebration and an official flag-off. We chatted and enjoyed the little warmth of the sun as we moved up in two groups, Group A and Group B. I was part of Group B, consisting of people with lesser experience and first-time trekkers like me. Our group leader instructed us not to speed up and stay in groups or pairs. My friend and I chose to stay at the tail end of the group to ensure that everyone was doing fine.

As we climbed, we helped people who needed support, took enough rest, and maintained a breezy pace. However, I was getting exhausted, and I used taking photographs as an excuse to take breaks in between. Eventually, we reached the last and set up our tents, but since we arrived last, we did not get the best location to put our tents.

On the second day of the trek, we were ascending from an altitude of 3000 meters to 4000 meters. As we moved up, I was being cautious and taking it slow. My friend and I were trailing behind the group, but we didn't mind as we are busy talking with some fellow trekkers.

After four hours of trekking, we realized that we were the last ones in the group, with only four people left behind us. Two of them were struggling with health issues, while the third was my friend. The fourth person was our group leader or coach, who urged me to move ahead while he stayed behind with the others. However, before he asked me to continue, he gave me a motivating pep talk to boost my morale.

I handed over my camera bag to one of the porters a little ahead of me and resumed my climb. Despite the physical strain, I am determined to keep going and reach the destination.

On the way back from the peak, I felt a different energy inside of me. I had partnered with a new friend who shared my interest in photography, and we chatted and took pictures together. Our speed was impressive, and we were the fastest in our group B and faster than many in group A as well.

When I returned to my tent and reflected on the day, I realized that I had been carrying a preconceived notion that the climb would be so steep that even the locals would struggle with it. This idea, along with the fact that I was a new trekker and needed to be cautious, had filled my knowledge bag. It made my trek up to the next point so difficult that it became worrisome for the group leaders and potters to match and take care of the 20-30 people who were climbing at their own pace.

This experience made me realize that sometimes, we need to empty our knowledge bags to make room for new ideas and experiences. The idea that the climb would be too steep was something I had picked up along the way, and it had influenced my thinking and made the trek more challenging than it needed to be.

As we go through life, we accumulate knowledge and experiences that shape our perceptions and beliefs. However, sometimes these beliefs can become limiting, holding us back from experiencing new things and achieving our goals. In my case, the preconceived notion about the climb had limited my ability to enjoy the trek and partner with others who shared my interests.

By emptying our knowledge bags, we can let go of limiting beliefs and open ourselves up to new ideas and experiences. It requires us to be open-minded,

willing to challenge our assumptions and embrace new perspectives. In doing so, we can unlock our full potential and achieve our goals.

Unlearn to learn

The journey of life is like a vast ocean, and we are all sailors on this journey. The ocean can be treacherous at times, with rough waters and unexpected storms, but it can also be a source of great adventure and discovery. To navigate this journey successfully, we need to learn the skills necessary to overcome obstacles and steer our course towards our goals.

Learning should be easy, right? Since we have been learning ever since we were born, we are picking up new things and making them a part of our own self. We have learnt so many things academic-wise, which brought us here to this point where we can say we are somewhat successful and leading a more than decent life, barring a few challenges here and there but we are OK with our lives.

Learning has never been this easy, with so much information and knowledge being available at our finger tips. Unlike a few decades ago when people could learn things only by books, teachers, trainers, or friends and guides. Now with the internet and technology giving us access to tap into any form of knowledge has become so much easy. Even toddlers were attending their prep classes on-line during the lockdown, and senior scientist, researchers can connect with fellows anywhere in the world to exchange notes and collaborate to bring out new innovations and theories.

So, despite all of the conveniences provided by this sector, why does studying appear to be a burden? Why do we make the excuse that we have fallen out of the habit of studying?

People like you and me often find it difficult to pick up new skills or learn new things. We are already preoccupied with so many things in our lives and have responsibilities, which puts our desire to learn something new on a back seat and rarely shows up on our priority list. We may be responsible for a family, a mortgage, and a stressful job. As a result, they may have less time and energy to devote to learning new things. We simply label this as a lack of time and energy.

Another reason why people may find it difficult to learn new things is because they are **afraid of rocking the boat** in their current situation. It can be particularly true in professional settings. Some professionals are hesitant to try new things or take on new challenges. They fear upsetting the status quo or damaging their relationships with colleagues or superiors.

In many workplaces, there can be a culture of conformity, where individuals are expected to fit into a certain mold and not deviate from established norms or procedures. It can create a sense of inertia, where individuals feel trapped in their current roles and are afraid to take risks or try new approaches.

Moreover, individuals may also fear losing their job or position if they fail to perform at their usual level. This fear can be particularly acute in industries that are experiencing rapid change or disruption. Individuals may feel that their skills and knowledge are becoming obsolete.

However, it is critical to recognize that taking risks and trying new things can lead to new opportunities and growth. By stepping outside of their comfort zone and challenging themselves to learn new skills or approaches, individuals may be able to enhance their value to their employer, build new connections, and open up new career pathways.

One of the key factors that contribute to cognitive decline with age is the natural aging process of the brain. As we age, our brain undergoes structural and functional changes that can affect our ability to learn and retain new information. The brain also experiences a gradual decline in the production of certain chemicals crucial for memory and cognitive function.

In addition, chronic stress and other health conditions can also play a role in cognitive decline. Stress can cause damage to the brain, leading to memory loss and other cognitive problems. Other health conditions such as dementia and Alzheimer's disease can also impact on cognitive function.

It is important to note that not everyone experiences cognitive decline with age. Lifestyle factors such as regular exercise, a healthy diet, and social engagement can help to preserve cognitive function in older adults. Engaging in mentally stimulating activities, such as learning a new language or playing brain games, can also help to keep the brain active and healthy.

There are a few interesting mindset-related reasons that act as obstacle to learning new things.

1. Fear of failure
2. Fixed mindset
3. Familiarity bias

Fear of failure is a common experience that can be a major obstacle to learning new things, especially as people get older. As we age, we tend to become more risk-averse. It can lead to a reluctance to try new things or take on new challenges. Fear of failure can manifest in many different ways, such as anxiety, self-doubt, and a lack of confidence.

One of the main reasons why people may experience fear of failure is the worry about looking foolish or making mistakes. It can be particularly true in social situations, where people may be afraid of being judged or ridiculed by others. In professional settings, fear of failure can be even more acute, as mistakes or failures can have serious consequences for one's career or reputation.

Another reason why people may experience fear of failure is the belief that failure is a reflection of their personal worth or intelligence. This type of thinking can lead to a fixed mindset, which is the belief that one's abilities and intelligence are set and cannot be improved. It can be a major obstacle to learning new things, as it can create a sense of complacency and limit an individual's potential for growth and development.

The good news is that fear of failure is not a permanent state of mind. With effort and practice, individuals can develop strategies to overcome their fears and take on new challenges. One approach is to focus on the process of learning, rather than the outcome. Instead of worrying about whether they will be successful or not, individuals can focus on the effort they put in and the progress they make over time. By viewing mistakes and setbacks as opportunities for learning and growth, individuals can develop resilience and a willingness to take on new challenges.

Another approach to overcoming the fear of failure is to practice self-compassion. This involves treating oneself with kindness and understanding, rather than being self-critical. By acknowledging that everyone makes mistakes and experiences failure at some point in their lives, individuals can reduce their fear of failure and develop a more positive and supportive mindset.

No, I am not encouraging you to make mistakes. All I am saying here is that every mistake is a learning opportunity. Rather if one is bound to mistakes, one should try and make new mistakes. That is a reflection of trying out new ways of working. All leading to reach that objective.

A fixed mindset is a belief that an individual's abilities and intelligence are static, and cannot be improved or changed. This mindset can be a major barrier to learning new skills or trying new things. It can create a sense of complacency and limit an individual's potential for growth and development.

People with a fixed mindset may be resistant to taking on new challenges or seeking out new experiences because they believe that their abilities are set and cannot be improved. They may be afraid of failure or looking foolish and may avoid situations that require them to stretch their skills or take risks. It can lead to a lack of personal and professional growth, as well as missed opportunities for learning and development.

It's reassuring that having a fixed mindset is not a permanent condition of thinking. By investing effort and practice, people can cultivate a growth mindset, which is the conviction that their skills and intelligence can improve through persistence, devotion, and hard work.

Familiarity bias is when we prefer what's familiar and comfortable over what's new. It affects our ability to learn new things, especially as we get older and become set in our ways.

As we accumulate knowledge and experience, we become more confident in our beliefs and less willing to consider new perspectives. It makes it challenging to embrace new ideas different from what we're used to.

We tend to seek information that confirms our beliefs and avoid information that challenges them. It reinforces familiarity bias and makes it hard to learn new things that go against our beliefs.

Empty Your Bags. Unlock Your Potential.

This bias reinforces our existing beliefs and can create an echo chamber where we only consume information that aligns with our opinions. It narrows our worldview and limits our ability to understand others.

In today's world, we have easy access to information that confirms our beliefs, making it easy to ignore alternative viewpoints. This confirmation bias strengthens stereotypes and prejudices, preventing us from empathizing with others.

Familiarity bias has serious consequences. It hinders personal and professional growth, limits our adaptability, and hampers creative problem-solving. It also hinders our ability to collaborate with people who think differently.

Middle-aged individuals face additional challenges in overcoming familiarity bias. They have established ways of thinking and may feel they have less time and energy to learn. Aging can also affect cognitive abilities, making it harder to absorb new information.

However, it's possible to overcome familiarity bias and continue learning throughout life. Adopting a growth mindset and seeking new experiences can help. Challenging existing beliefs and exposing ourselves to diverse perspectives broaden our knowledge and help us adapt to change.

Have you ever found yourself in a situation where you are attending a business presentation, training session, or even a social gathering, and you feel like you already know what the other person is going to say? This feeling of disinterest and disconnection is all too common, and I have personally experienced it many times in my life.

This feeling of detachment and lack of enthusiasm is a particular hurdle in the business world. As part of the corporate world, I'm constantly listening to the same topics discussed in meetings and presentations. As I sit in the same meeting day after day, I find my thoughts wandering and my attention fading. That might block me from a favorable opportunity.

This feeling of disinterest and disconnection can be particularly challenging in business settings. As someone who works in the corporate world, I attend many meetings and presentations that cover similar topics. At times, it feels like I am attending the same meeting over and over again, and my mind begins to tune out.

This feeling of disinterest and disconnection can also occur in social situations. When we meet new people, we often fall into the trap of making assumptions about them based on their appearance or the context in which we meet them. We may assume that we know what they are going to say or how they are going to act, which can lead to disinterest and disconnection.

However, it is essential to recognize that this feeling of disinterest and disconnection is not a reflection of the other person or their message. Instead, it reflects our own mindset and approach to learning and growth.

Empty Your Bags. Unlock Your Potential.

When we approach any situation with an open mind and a willingness to learn, we are more likely to stay engaged and present. We can challenge ourselves to look for new insights and perspectives, even if we feel like we already know the material. We can ask questions and seek clarification, rather than assuming that we already know the answer.

That is the reason I suggest we empty our KNOWLEDGE bag, what we already know, which will make space for new learnings.

Let's take the example of my friend who was discussing where to settle for her later years in life. She had traveled around the world and had the financial means to live anywhere in her home country. However, she chose to live in a big city so that she would have access to medical help in case of any health emergencies that may arise with age. While her decision was logical, it also made me think about the importance of planning for the long-term and making decisions that align with our desires and values.

My reply to her was obviously one should plan things in detail, but have you thought if you move to a peaceful place up in the Himalayas, where your heart lies, which will any way add those extra years to your life and reduce the tendency to fall sick.

I suggested to my friend that she should consider her personal preferences and values when deciding where to settle. While living in a big city may provide easy access to medical care, it may not necessarily align with her desire to live in a peaceful place. Moving to a place like the Himalayas, where her heart lies, could potentially add extra years to her life and reduce the tendency to fall sick.

Keep sharpening your saw

Developing skills and abilities can have a significant impact on our daily lives. When we acquire new skills and knowledge, we become better equipped to handle different situations, whether it's managing our finances, fixing a leaky faucet, or learning a new language. By doing so, we can reduce the burden of carrying around the weight of our daily problems and responsibilities, allowing us to live a simpler and more efficient life.

Learning how to manage with available resources is also an essential skill that can help us lighten our load. By using what we have at hand, we can avoid accumulating unnecessary possessions and reduce our environmental impact. For example, by learning how to cook simple and healthy meals using local, seasonal ingredients, we can avoid buying expensive and unhealthy fast food, reduce waste, and save money.

Moreover, developing skills and abilities can also help us become more self-sufficient and independent, giving us the confidence and ability to handle different situations on our own. Whether it's changing a tire, fixing a broken appliance, or navigating a new city, having the skills and knowledge to do so can make our journeys more comfortable and enjoyable.

My experience of developing new skills during a trek. While trekking with a group of professional trekkers and mountain climbers, I was surprised to find that they had set up multiple video calls with the trekking group before the trek to prepare everyone. Initially, I did not take the preparation too seriously, but later on, I was included in the calls and given downloads from previous conversations.

During the preparation, the group leaders made the group prepare a list of things to get and walk every day with increasing step counts, including walking with the backpacks and shoes that we will be carrying with us on the mountain trek. This helped me to develop a new habit of walking daily with heavy shoes, which proved to be beneficial in the trek.

As I walked with increasing weight and distance, I found myself becoming more confident and capable of facing the challenges of the trek. The new skill I developed helped me in walking in my shoes and carrying some weight at the height of 4000 meters, bringing me closer to achieving my dream.

This experience highlighted the importance of preparation and training, even for experienced trekkers, and the benefits of developing new skills and habits in pursuit of one's goals.

Empty Your Bags. Unlock Your Potential.

As a creative director in the field of graphic design, my professional journey has involved a constant process of unlearning and learning new things to keep up with the ever-evolving landscape of design and technology. This experience of developing new skills during a trek further reinforced the importance of being open to new ideas and approaches.

The preparation and training that the group leaders provided before the trek demonstrated the value of unlearning old habits and developing new ones. Walking daily with heavy shoes and increasing weight helped me build the stamina and confidence necessary to overcome the challenges of the trek. This experience taught me that embracing new skills and habits is essential to achieving one's goals, even for experienced professionals.

As a creative director, I explore various innovative techniques and technologies to push beyond my comfort zone. By letting go of old habits and embracing more innovative approaches, I can create innovative solutions that stand out in a constantly evolving industry.

A few years ago, while shopping with my family, I found myself with some free time while my wife browsed the women's clothing section. To keep my 10-year-old daughter entertained, I took out my phone and showed her some pictures and videos from a recent trip we had taken. Then, an idea struck me to make a short video using a smartphone app that compiles our photos and videos with music and transitions. In just 10 minutes, I created a quick video that my daughter loved. With my guidance, she could make another one in 10-15 minutes.

It was impressive to see how easily my daughter adapted to advancing technology and how quickly she could create something that would have taken me days to do a few years ago. As someone who learned video editing the arduous way, I recognized the value of adapting to new technology and techniques. It's essential to let go of old mindsets and embrace more innovative ways to stay relevant in today's fast-paced industry.

When working with younger designers, I notice that they often rely on easier tools and available resources. This can make them more productive than those who learn the hard way. But, I still believe there is value in extra effort and learning new skills. It's imperative to strike a balance between utilizing the latest technology and putting in the right amount of work to develop abilities.

The key to success in any industry is to continually explore evolving techniques and technologies while unlearning old habits and embracing more innovative approaches. By doing so, one can create innovative solutions and stand out in a constantly evolving industry.

Empty Your Bags. Unlock Your Potential.

It is important to **empty your knowledge bag**—empty of all we already know, and know about our capabilities.

Once the knowledge bag gets emptied, it has some scope for adding new skills and learning, which could help us achieve our dreams.

Exercise:

List down the new skills and learning you picked up in last 6 months to one year time frame by unlearning what you already knew.

_____

_____

_____

And don't forget to celebrate what you learnt new in direction of fulfilling your dreams.

Ajay Rawat

What's taking up the space

The Journey of Life: Understanding the concept of carrying less

I got all the required items for my trek and struggled to fit them in a single bag. And until I checked into the airplane, I kept my fingers crossed that it would not go over the permissible limits. And I kept wondering: What all did I pack in the bag—did I go a little over, or is it OK? Thankfully my luggage weight was just under the permissible limits and rest of the plane journey was nice.

On our journey through life, when we are walking towards our dreams with our new capabilities, do we know what is filling up our mind space?

As we commence on the journey of life, it's natural to think about what we should carry with us. When planning a trip to the mountains in the middle of winter, for example, the list of necessary items can be long. Warm clothing, waterproof gear, food and water, a light source, proper footwear, medicine, and more - the list goes on. But, we have discussed about Buddhist monks on the top of a mountain, calmly meditating without any clothes, with only a damp cloth wrapped around their body to keep them warm. It's a remarkable sight, one that makes us question the number of things we think we need to survive and be comfortable in the face of extreme conditions.

Empty Your Bags. Unlock Your Potential.

The brain's desire to accumulate more and more is influenced by both evolutionary and cultural factors. Evolution has made the human brain highly sensitive to potential dangers and opportunities in the environment, causing it to develop a strong urge to accumulate resources. This urge has been crucial for survival throughout human history and helped individuals build reserves for difficult times.

However, in modern society, this accumulation drive has taken on a new form, with individuals accumulating more possessions than necessary for their basic needs. This shift is due to cultural factors such as consumerism, which values material goods and encourages individuals to buy more.

The brain's reward system also contributes to this accumulation drive. The brain experiences pleasure and satisfaction when it acquires resources or possessions, and this feeling is reinforced by the release of dopamine in the brain. This creates a cycle where individuals seek out new experiences and possessions in search of pleasure and satisfaction.

As you must have known our brain get the sense of pleasure by release of Dopamine hormone, which is commonly known as the reward hormone. This release of dopamine creates a pleasurable or reinforcing sensation that can motivate us to repeat the behavior that led to the reward.

Consuming a flavorful dish can create a positive experience in the brain, thus releasing dopamine and sparking feelings of reward. This type of gratification encourages us to look for similar foods and flavors in subsequent meals.

When we acquire something new or accomplish a goal, dopamine is released, creating a positive reinforcement that encourages us to repeat the behavior.

Additionally, the prefrontal cortex of our brain, which is responsible for decision-making and planning, also plays a role in accumulation. The prefrontal cortex allows us to weigh the costs and benefits of acquiring something new and helps us plan for the future.

Excessive acquisition of goods can lead to hoarding behavior. This behavior may be linked with changes in the brain's reward system and levels of prefrontal cortex activity, creating a distorted perception on the value of objects as well as difficulty in making decisions regarding retention and disposal.

Hoarding is a condition characterized by the excessive accumulation of possessions and the inability to discard them, regardless of their actual value or usefulness. The behavior often leads to cluttered living spaces that can become hazardous to the person's health and safety.

Researchers have found that hoarding behavior is linked to alterations in the brain's reward system and prefrontal cortex. The reward system, which involves the release of dopamine in response to pleasurable experiences, can become dysregulated in individuals with hoarding disorder. This means that the brain's reward center may be more sensitive to the acquisition of objects, leading to an exaggerated feeling of pleasure and reinforcement.

Furthermore, the prefrontal cortex, which is responsible for decision-making and executive function, may also be affected in individuals with hoarding disorder. This can result in difficulty in making decisions about what to keep and what to discard, as well as difficulty in organizing and planning.

Research has also shown that hoarding behavior may be linked to underlying emotional and psychological factors, such as anxiety, depression, and trauma. These factors may contribute to the compulsive acquisition and retention of objects, as a way of coping with emotional distress or feelings of insecurity.

The monk's ability to meditate without clothes in the middle of winter on a snow-covered mountain is a testament to their inner strength. They have developed their bodies and minds to a level that they can withstand the cold and keep themselves warm, to the extent that they can raise the temperatures enough to steam the damp cloth that covers their bodies. This is an example of how a few people have achieved comfort and peace of mind by developing their inner power, as opposed to relying on external possessions.

In the same vein, simplification can play a role in our journey through life. By reducing the number of possessions and distractions in our lives, we can focus on what truly matters and develop our inner strength to achieve our goals in a more focused and sustainable way. As we delve deeper into the concept of simplification, we will explore how it can help us achieve our goals in a more focused and intentional way, how aligning our actions with our values can lead to greater success and happiness, and how building supportive relationships and partnerships can help us achieve our ambitious goals.

It's all about brain

Our brain is a special organ and has special abilities to store information, we keep collecting information to learn new things and we intentionally memorize things. But memories are different than what we memorize contextually. Our memories influence how we think, speak, and act, in short, how we behave. Some memories are wonderful, some are not so good, and some are horrible. The not-so-good and dreadful ones cause us emotional distress and, at times, manifest physically.

It becomes tricky to manage or deal with your memories, they occupy some space in our brain. However, when I say declutter your brain, I mean more than just dealing with a particular memory. According to current study, memories in the human brain are stored in more than one location. In the study of memory, and argues that memories are stored in multiple regions of the brain, each contributing to different aspects of the memory. The authors argue that their multiple trace model provides a more accurate representation of human memory than traditional models and has important implications for our understanding of the neural basis of memory.

The multiple trace model of memory is based on the idea that memories are stored in multiple regions of the brain, each contributing to different aspects of the memory. According to this model, memories are stored in the form of multiple traces, each representing a different aspect of the memory, such as sensory information, emotional content, and context. The multiple traces are stored in different regions of the brain, such as the hippocampus, the amygdala, and the neocortex, and are thought to interact with one another to support memory storage and retrieval.

One of the key insights from this research is that the different regions of the brain that store different aspects of a memory can be acivated separately, allowing for the retrieval of different aspects of a memory at different times. This has important implications for our understanding of memory retrieval, as it suggests that different aspects of a memory can be retrieved separately, depending on the information that is needed.

The authors provide evidence for the multiple trace model from a variety of sources, including studies of brain-damaged patients and from studies using neuroimaging techniques. They argue that this evidence supports the multiple trace model and demonstrates its superiority over traditional models of memory storage.

One of the most compelling pieces of evidence for the multiple trace model comes from studies of patients with brain damage. The authors argue that these studies demonstrate that different aspects of memory can be selectively lost, depending on the location of the brain damage. For example, patients with damage to the hippocampus often have difficulty remembering the context of events, while patients with damage to the amygdala have difficulty remembering the emotional content of events.

Another important piece of evidence comes from studies using neuroimaging techniques, such as functional Magnetic Resonance Imaging (fMRI) and Positron Emission Tomography (PET). These studies have shown that different regions of the brain are activated during the retrieval of different aspects of a memory. For example, the hippocampus is activated when the context of a memory is retrieved, while the amygdala is activated when the emotional content of a memory is retrieved.

The authors argue that the multiple trace model of memory has important implications for our understanding of the neural basis of memory. They argue that this model provides a more accurate representation of how memories are stored and retrieved in the human brain, and that it has important implications for our understanding of the relationship between brain regions and memory.

When it comes to good and bad memories, the emotional content of the memory is thought to be processed and stored in the Amygdala, a region of the brain involved in processing emotions. Research has shown that the amygdala is more active when people are processing emotionally charged memories, such as those of a traumatic event, compared to neutral memories.

Additionally, the context in which a memory was formed can also affect its storage. For example, research has shown that the Hippocampus, a region of the brain involved in processing spatial information, is more active when people are forming and recalling memories in a specific context, such as a particular location.

Clutter in your head can give you a feeling of being overwhelmed, which is a common experience that many of us are all too familiar with. It's that moment when our brains feel overloaded with information, making it difficult to process, organize and make decisions. This can lead to physical symptoms such as stress, headaches and other forms of discomfort. To cope, some people turn to comfort food, drinks or even smokes as a temporary escape.

From a neurobiological perspective, being overwhelmed can result from an overstimulation of the amygdala, a region of the brain involved in processing emotions, particularly negative emotions like fear and anxiety. When the amygdala is overstimulated, it can trigger a release of stress hormones, such as Cortisol, which can result in feelings of overwhelm.

From a cognitive perspective, being overwhelmed can result from an inability to manage and process information effectively. When we are faced with too much information or too many demands, our cognitive resources can become depleted, leading to feelings of overwhelm.

Empty Your Bags. Unlock Your Potential.

From a psychological perspective, being overwhelmed can result from a sense of loss of control or a perceived lack of ability to handle a situation. When we feel that we are unable to cope with the demands being placed on us, this can lead to feelings of overwhelm.

We've witnessed the intricate and interconnected nature of brain structure and functioning, where multiple locations store various types of information along with their respective contextual details. It's no surprise that the feeling of being overwhelmed easily creeps in, as this extensive network of storage takes up space in our brain, impacting our amygdala and subsequently influencing our decision-making process.

- - - - - - - - - -

When friends come to me with similar struggles, I suggest they take a moment to sit down, take a deep breath and identify the areas that require their immediate attention. The key is to approach the situation objectively and without any added negative experiences, like thinking that a task is too difficult or painful to undertake. More often than not, my friends have reported feeling better and taking improved actions.

I, too, have faced moments of feeling overwhelmed and find that organizing my surroundings can help. When I'm dealing with clutter in my head, whether it's from random, unnecessary thoughts or from feeling guilty or regretful about something, I find it helpful to put things in order and align them visually. This helps to reduce my stress levels and gives me a clearer view of the situation.

Everyone has their own ways of dealing with the feeling of being overwhelmed. Whether it's through organizing, deep breathing, writing or other means, it's important to have techniques that help us regain control and bring peace to our minds. Remember, taking control of our thoughts and surroundings can lead to a more fulfilling and productive life.

Take out 5 minutes and write down your ways to declutter your surroundings and your mind.

_____

_____

_____

Let's examine the idea of simplification and its connection to the journey of life. By reducing the amount, we carry, both physically and mentally, we can focus on what truly matters and live a more fulfilling and intentional existence. We will see how a minimalist and simple approach to life can help us achieve our goals in a more focused and sustainable way, and how it can foster stronger connections and collaborations.

Empty Your Bags. Unlock Your Potential.

So, come along as we explore the power of simplification, and why less is truly more.

The idea of having a choice between accumulating physical possessions and giving them up to develop inner strength is a crucial one to consider. In the example of climbing high mountains in snowy winters, a person may initially pack and carry a vast array of items to ensure their survival, including warm clothing, food, water, medicine, and various tools. In contrast Tibbetian monks who are able to meditate in the harsh, extreme conditions without any physical protection, it brings to light the power of inner strength and the choice to accumulate material possessions or develop something much more profound.

This highlights how one can choose to focus on external factors for survival and comfort, or turn inward to cultivate the power of the mind and spirit. The monk's ability to generate warmth and comfort from within, even in the face of inhospitable conditions, is a testament to the strength of the inner self.

Therefore, this example serves as a reminder that one can choose to accumulate material possessions in pursuit of comfort and security, or develop something far more valuable and long-lasting - the power of the mind and spirit. In doing so, one can find greater satisfaction, happiness, and fulfillment on the journey of life.

Ajay Rawat

Less is more

Diogenes of Sinope was an influential philosopher in ancient Greece, renowned for his unique philosophy of Cynicism. He was a firm believer in leading a life of minimalism and asceticism, rejecting materialistic desires and the conventions of society. To embody his beliefs, Diogenes lived with very basic means, residing in a barrel that was his only home, with only a few rags and a drinking cup for necessities. Despite his simple living arrangements, he was a well-known figure in Athens, frequently engaging in philosophical discussions and beguiling onlookers with his wit and unorthodox behavior.

One of the most famous stories about Diogenes involves the time he saw a young child drinking water by cupping his hands. This moment had a profound impact on him, as he realized that even a child possessed a wisdom and understanding of minimalism that he himself had yet to achieve. Overcome with emotion, he immediately discarded his only drinking cup, symbolizing his newfound commitment to a life of simplicity and self-sufficiency. This story has become an iconic representation of Diogenes' philosophy of Cynicism, and continues to inspire individuals who seek to live an authentic and meaningful life, free from the trappings of material possessions and societal norms.

Empty Your Bags. Unlock Your Potential.

The concept of carrying less is not limited to just philosophers or those seeking a minimalist lifestyle. In fact, many financially savvy individuals have also recognized the benefits of owning and maintaining fewer possessions. One example is a wealthy individual who owned a billion-dollar mansion, spending millions to maintain it. Eventually, the person realized the excessive outflow of money just to maintain the asset, prompting them to sell it off and move into a five-star hotel. By paying a premium to stay in the hotel for several years, they now have the best living accommodations with all of the hotel staff at their disposal.

The idea of carrying less can apply to any aspect of life, not just material possessions. It can also include reducing unnecessary tasks and activities that do not add value or contribute to personal growth. The philosophy behind carrying less is to simplify one's life, reduce clutter, and focus on what truly matters. By letting go of excess baggage, individuals can achieve greater clarity and focus on their priorities.

Carrying less can also have financial benefits, as in the case of the wealthy individual who sold their mansion. By reducing the number of possessions and assets one owns, the expenses associated with their upkeep also decrease. This, in turn, can lead to a more cost-effective and efficient lifestyle. Additionally, owning fewer possessions can reduce the need for larger living spaces or storage units, which can further reduce expenses.

Ajay Rawat

Carrying less is a very important aspect in design and creative, which translate to "less is more". Carrying less is a very important aspect of art and design, which translates to "less is more". This design philosophy can be a minor but powerful signifier between someone new to the field and a seasoned professional in our creative field.

In design and creativity, "less is more" is an essential principle that stresses the power of minimalism and simplicity. By carefully analyzing the design elements and removing any redundant details, a professional can design a balanced, powerful visual that will draw in the viewers and keep their curiosity alive.

The psychological impact of this approach on an individual is equally significant. The designer can use the right amount of information to lure the viewer into solving a puzzle. To marvel at the intelligence and skill put into creating the artwork, and to acknowledge the depth behind the beauty of its simple composition. On the contrary, an overly complicated or busy design can perplex the spectator, resulting in a lack of interest or disengagement.

The essential rule of "less is more" can help creators and designers improve the quality of their work and create more captivating and unforgettable results. It's a careful balance of giving the viewer enough information to catch their eye and leaving enough for them to explore and give their own interpretation of the design. To master this concept, you need to have experience, skill, and knowledge of the audience's wants, likes, and expectations. The result is a design that is classic, stylish, and captivating, going beyond fashion and trends.

There is this short video getting popular on social media, featuring a monkey who keeping grabbing food and not eating it. This showcases humans, like monkeys, often tend to hoard things without considering their actual needs. Just as the monkey keeps grabbing the bread without taking the time to eat it, humans tend to accumulate possessions without taking the time to enjoy them. This results in a clutter of items that may never be used or appreciated.

The analogy between the monkey's behavior and human behavior highlights the tendency for humans to focus on acquiring more, rather than taking the time to enjoy what they already have. This often leads to a sense of dissatisfaction and a constant desire for more.

It is important to recognize this tendency and make conscious efforts to break away from it. Instead of constantly striving for more, it is crucial to take stock of what we already have and appreciate it. This can bring a sense of contentment and fulfillment that cannot be achieved through accumulation alone. Humans possess a distinctive characteristic that sets us apart from other species, the tendency to accumulate possessions. Regardless of the amount we already own, we continuously add to our collection, driven by a desire to provide for ourselves, our family, and our loved ones. However, as we become consumed with the act of accumulation, we fail to recognize that we are missing out on the opportunity to enjoy the fruits of our labor. Our focus becomes solely on the future, causing us to neglect the present moment and our connection with the world around us.

The preoccupation with accumulating often limits our ability to experience life fully and connect with nature, which has the power to rejuvenate and renew. We become so consumed with material possessions that we forget the simple pleasures in life, such as the beauty of a sunset or the peace of a quiet walk in nature. The pursuit of material wealth can often lead to a sense of emptiness and dissatisfaction, as we struggle to find happiness and fulfillment through material gains.

"The things you own end up owning you"

- Chuck Palahniuk

This quote by Chuck Palahniuk highlights the grim reality of the trap we are weaving for ourselves. It is importance to strike a balance between material possessions and finding true freedom in life. By giving up our attachment to material goods and seeking meaningful experiences and connections, we can tap into a source of power and happiness that is greater than anything money can buy. We live in a world that often glorifies material wealth, but the truth is that true contentment can only be found by embracing the present moment and connecting with the natural world around us. By doing so, we can free ourselves from the constraints of consumerism and find a deeper sense of purpose and fulfillment in life. In short, we must strive to find a balance between our material desires and our need for meaningful experiences and connections, and in doing so, we can truly own our lives, rather than being owned by our possessions.

Ajay Rawat

Mental Models and Philosophies: Simplify for a fulfilling life

Numerous philosophers, scientists, thinkers, and enlightened individuals have dedicated their lives to comprehending human behavior, striving to uncover the motivations behind our actions. Throughout history, they have put forth a range of mental models, principles, and lifestyles that aim to offer guidance and insight in the intricate and constantly evolving realm of human existence.

From the ancient Greeks to modern-day researchers, there have been countless attempts to explain human behavior. Some philosophers have argued that human behavior is determined by reason and rational thought, while others have proposed that behavior is driven by emotions and instincts. Scientists have attempted to understand behavior through various disciplines such as psychology, biology, and neuroscience, among others. Meanwhile, spiritual and enlightened individuals have offered insights into the nature of human consciousness and how it affects behavior.

These models and principles offer insights into human motivation, decision-making, and the pursuit of meaning and purpose. Additionally, some of these individuals have proposed different ways of living that aim to promote personal growth, self-awareness, and a sense of fulfillment. By exploring these mental models, principles, and ways of living, individuals can gain a deeper understanding of themselves and the world around them, and ultimately live more meaningful and fulfilling lives.

As human beings, it's easy to become overwhelmed by life's complexities; the constant pursuit of materialistic security, or the need for relationships, or even for self-fulfilment. To clarify the confusion, the American psychologist **Abraham Maslow** proposed the **Hierarchy of Needs** - a basic framework which suggests that human needs can be divided into five distinct categories, each of which must be fulfilled before progressing to the next. For a fulfilled life, these needs must be taken in order of importance.

The first tier, physiological needs, include the fundamental requirements for human survival. These are basic needs based on physiology, including access to food, water, shelter and clothing.

The second tier, safety needs, are those which create an environment of stability and security. These include the formation of methodical routines, a secure job

and living situation and a sense of safety in both oneself and their external environment.

The third tier is related to social needs, or personal bonds which allow people to interact with one another. This includes family, relationships and friends. The fourth and fifth tiers of Maslow's Hierarchy of Needs are referred to as the "self-actualization" needs. They involve a striving for self-fulfilment and a need to grow. At this level, individuals seek to become more self-aware and to find their own particular purpose in life. They seek to discover their highest potentials and fulfill their individual needs. This could include activities such as pursuing knowledge and understanding their own capabilities, or seeking novel experiences, such as art, literature, music, and philosophy. Relationships are also important, as individuals strive to share their ideas and experiences with others and develop meaningful relationships. Self-actualization is key to a well-rounded, fulfilling life

Maslow's hierarchy of needs is a well-known theory that explains the progression of human needs from the most basic physiological needs, such as food and shelter, to the highest level of self-actualization. However, many individuals struggle to meet their needs and reach self-actualization due to an overwhelming focus on material possessions and consumerism. This is where a minimalistic approach to life can help. By simplifying one's life, individuals can focus on fulfilling their needs and reaching their full potential.

So, where do you stand on Maslow's Need Hierarchy?

Take a moment to reflect on your current needs and wants. Are your physiological needs being met, or are you struggling to meet your basic needs for food, shelter, and clothing? If so, it is important to address these needs first before moving on to the next tier.

It is important to note that individuals may move up and down the pyramid at different times in their lives.

For example, an individual who is in the middle of a divorce may feel a stronger need for love and belonging, while someone who has just achieved a major accomplishment may feel a stronger need for esteem and recognition.

As you reflect on your current position in the hierarchy, consider the steps you can take to fulfill your needs. For example, if you feel a strong need for self-actualization, consider what changes you need to make in your life in order to reach your full potential. On the other hand, if you feel lonely and isolated, consider reaching out to friends and loved ones, or taking steps to become involved in your community.

Maslow's Need Hierarchy is just an observation but still powerful way to look at personal growth and self-discovery. By reflecting on your current needs and wants, you can gain a better understanding of what is truly important to you, and what steps you need to take in order to fulfill those needs. So, ask yourself, what tier are you on, and are you ready to move to the next level?

The Pareto principle, also known as the 80/20 rule, which states that roughly 80% of effects come from 20% of causes. This principle is often used in business and economics to understand the distribution of wealth or the importance of certain customers or products. Often this is referred to motivate people to come in the 20% people of the world who owns 80% of world's wealth.

The Pareto Principle, or the 80/20 rule, is a concept that can be applied to a variety of areas in life, from business to personal productivity. The principle states that 80% of results or outcomes come from 20% of efforts or causes. For example, in a business setting, 80% of sales might come from 20% of customers, or 80% of profits might come from 20% of products. In personal productivity, the principle suggests that 80% of our success can be attributed to 20% of our efforts. In the last mention of 20% effort, I mean focus all your efforts on 20% option or direction instead of trying out anything and everything that wastes 80% of the effort. I invite you to look at this 80/20 rule a little differently.

In the context of minimalism, the Pareto Principle can help us identify the essential items in our lives and eliminate the excess. By applying the principle to our possessions, we can focus on the 20% of items that bring us the most value and let go of the remaining 80% that only contribute to clutter and distraction. This can lead to a more intentional and fulfilling life, as we are able to prioritize the things that truly matter and eliminate the excess that weighs us down.

The 80/20 rule can also be applied to other areas of minimalism, such as time management and relationships. By identifying the 20% of activities that bring us the most joy or productivity and eliminating the rest, we can create more space in our lives for the things that matter. In relationships, the principle suggests that 80% of our happiness and fulfillment comes from 20% of our connections, so we can focus on nurturing those relationships and letting go of the ones that no longer serve us.

The 80/20 principle applies to relationships as well: research shows that 80% of our happiness and fulfillment comes from the 20% of our connections which are the most important. The conclusion, then, is that it's worth investing in these relationships, while dropping those which are no longer productive or beneficial.

Overall, the Pareto Principle is a powerful tool for minimalists who want to simplify their lives and focus on what truly matters. By identifying the essential 20% of our possessions, activities, and relationships, we can create a life that is intentional, fulfilling, and free from the excess that can weigh us down.

Stoicism is a philosophical school of thought that originated in Athens, Greece, in the early 3rd century BC. It was founded by the philosopher Zeno of Citium, who taught his students to live a virtuous life through reason and self-control, even in the face of adversity. Stoicism emphasizes the importance of simplifying one's life and focusing on what is truly important. According to Stoicism, individuals should prioritize their values and focus on the present moment. This helps to cultivate ataraxia, a sense of inner peace, even in the face of adversity. Stoicism encourages individuals to be mindful of their thoughts and emotions, and to practice self-control in order to maintain a balanced and peaceful state of mind.

The name "Stoicism" is derived from the Greek word "stoa," which means "porch" or "colonnade," where Zeno and his followers would meet to discuss their ideas.

Stoicism gained popularity in ancient Greece and Rome, and many notable figures such as the Roman emperor Marcus Aurelius and the statesman and philosopher Seneca were adherents of the philosophy.

The principles of Stoicism emphasize the importance of living in harmony with nature and accepting the world as it is, rather than constantly striving for material possessions or external validation. Stoics believe that individuals should focus on what they can control and let go of what they cannot. They also emphasize the importance of developing self-control, rational thinking, and moral virtue, which are the keys to living a fulfilling life.

Today, Stoicism continues to be studied and practiced by many individuals around the world, and its teachings have influenced a wide range of fields, including psychology, ethics, and self-help.

There is a famous quote from Stoic philosopher Marcus Aurelius, he wrote,

> *"You have power over your mind, not outside events. Realize this, and you will find strength."*

This quote highlights the importance of focusing on what is within one's control, and accepting what is not, in order to maintain a sense of inner peace and balance. By prioritizing their values, focusing on the present moment, and cultivating a sense of inner peace, individuals can live a fulfilling and meaningful life that is free from the distractions and worries of consumerism. Minimalism, as a lifestyle that emphasizes simplicity, aligns with Stoicism in many ways and can help individuals live a more intentional life.

Zen Buddhism, another popular philosophy emphasizes the importance of simplifying one's life and focusing on what is truly important. Zen Buddhism encourages individuals to focus on the present moment, let go of attachment to material possessions, and cultivate inner peace and mindfulness. By embracing a minimalist lifestyle, individuals can cultivate a deeper sense of fulfillment and inner peace.

One famous Zen Buddhist quote that embodies this philosophy is,

> "*Letting go of what you don't need,*
>
> *you make room for what you do.*"

This quote speaks to the idea that by letting go of material possessions and distractions, individuals can make room for the things that truly matter and bring them happiness and fulfillment.

Zen Buddhism also encourages individuals to practice mindfulness, or being present in each moment without judgment or distraction. This practice helps individuals to live in the moment, rather than being preoccupied with worries or regrets from the past or anxieties about the future. By focusing on the present, individuals can cultivate inner peace and contentment, regardless of their external circumstances.

Ultimately, the philosophy of Zen Buddhism and the embrace of a minimalist lifestyle can help individuals to live a more fulfilling and intentional life, focused on what truly matters and free from the distractions of consumerism and materialism.

Throughout history, many philosophers, scientists, thinkers, and spiritual leaders have attempted to understand human behavior and provide guidance for living a fulfilling life. Centuries before Abraham Maslow proposed his principles, the Hindu Vedic tradition had already established its understanding of human behavior and the pursuit of a fulfilling life. Philosophers, scientists, thinkers, and spiritual leaders in this ancient tradition delineated life into four stages known as "Ashrams," each with its specific responsibilities and spiritual focus. It is remarkable that these insights were developed and practiced long before Maslow introduced his hierarchy of needs pyramid, highlighting the rich historical and philosophical heritage of the Hindu Vedic tradition.

The first stage is Brahmacharya, where an individual focus on education, self-discipline, and spiritual development. The second stage, Grihastha, is the householder stage, where an individual is expected to marry, raise a family, and fulfill social and familial responsibilities while maintaining a spiritual practice. The third stage, Vanaprastha, is a time for contemplation and introspection, with a focus on spiritual pursuits. The final stage, Sannyasa, is a complete renunciation of worldly life with a focus on spiritual growth and self-realization.

While the last two stages suggest moving away from material possessions and pursuing a spiritual path, it's important to note that not everyone is expected to follow this path. The four ashrams serve as a framework for individuals to lead a balanced and fulfilling life, focusing on both material and spiritual pursuits, with an ultimate goal of spiritual growth and self-realization.

It's interesting to note that similar ideas can be found in practical approaches, such as the **Lean Start-up methodology**. The Lean Start-up methodology is a practical approach to entrepreneurship that has gained popularity in recent years. This methodology emphasizes the importance of simplifying one's approach, focusing on strengths, and eliminating distractions that do not support one's goals. In essence, the Lean Start-up methodology echoes the principles of the four ashrams, which suggest focusing on what is truly important to lead a fulfilling life.

At the core of the Lean Start-up methodology is the concept of "validated learning." This means that entrepreneurs should prioritize testing and learning over simply launching a product. By testing and refining a product based on customer feedback and data, entrepreneurs can create a successful product without wasting time, money, and resources on ideas that may not be viable.

The Lean Start-up methodology also emphasizes the importance of quick and continuous iteration. This means that entrepreneurs should be adaptable and open to changing customer needs, as well as be willing to pivot their product or approach as necessary. By being nimble and responsive to feedback, entrepreneurs can create a product that truly meets the needs of their customers.

By keeping the focus on what truly matters, the Lean Start-up methodology can help entrepreneurs save time, money, and resources by only working on what is necessary to achieve their goals. This approach encourages individuals to prioritize their strengths and eliminate distractions that do not support their goals, creating a more efficient and effective path to success.

Advocates of the Lean Start-up methodology also emphasize the importance of Minimum Viable Product (MVP) which means creating a simplified version of the product that still provides value to customers. This approach allows entrepreneurs to test their ideas and receive feedback early on, which can help guide further development.

In short, the Lean Start-up methodology encourages individuals to simplify their approach, focus on what truly matters, and prioritize testing and learning over launching a full product. By doing so, individuals can achieve their goals more efficiently and effectively.

Empty Your Bags. Unlock Your Potential.

Adopting a minimalist lifestyle involves intentionally simplifying one's possessions, activities, and priorities in order to focus on what truly matters. This aligns with the principles of Maslow's hierarchy of needs, which suggests that individuals must fulfill their basic physiological and safety needs before moving on to higher-level needs such as self-actualization. Similarly, the stoic philosophy emphasizes the importance of focusing on what is within one's control and not becoming attached to material possessions or external circumstances. Zen Buddhism emphasizes the importance of being present in the moment and cultivating a clear and calm mind.

The Lean Start-up methodology also supports a minimalist approach, encouraging entrepreneurs to focus on what is truly necessary to achieve their goals and eliminating distractions that do not support those goals. By adopting these principles and philosophies, individuals can live a more intentional and purposeful life, free from the distractions and clutter that can weigh them down.

A minimalist lifestyle can bring many benefits, including reduced stress, increased focus, and greater satisfaction with life. By intentionally simplifying their lives, individuals can also save time and resources that can be used to pursue their passions and goals. Overall, embracing the principles of minimalism and other related philosophies can lead to a more fulfilling and intentional life.

Ajay Rawat

Empty Your Bag Of Time

Leverage

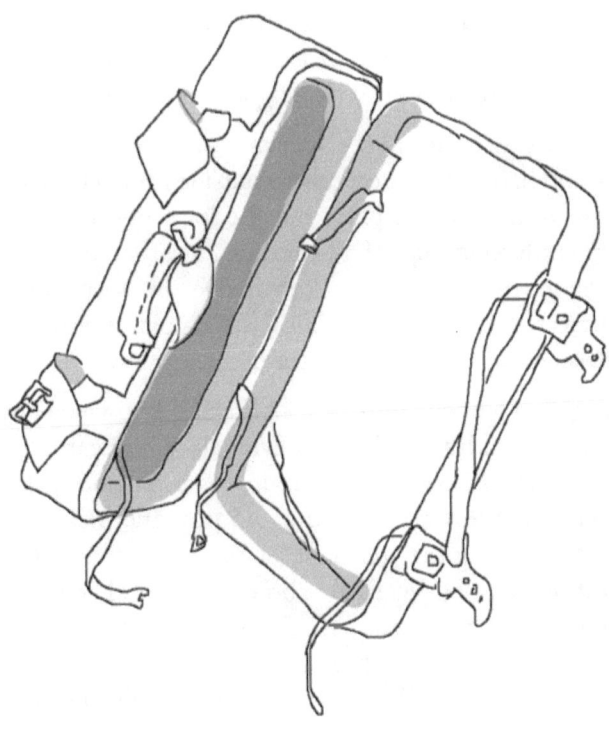

Empty Your Bags. Unlock Your Potential.

I decided to go on a trek where I will be meeting a bunch of individuals with who I never met or interacted before. The trek was led by experienced professional trekkers who had military training backgrounds. They have impressive credentials and carried out many successful expeditions. Still, they knew the importance of partnering with local climbers, guides, and trekkers. Their partnership with local people made all 25 of us cross the 4000-meter altitude mark and return safely with all good memories.

The trekking sector in the area we visited was relatively new and had opened recently to outside tourists like us. We were new to the place but the local people had a deep understanding of the terrain, weather patterns, available resources, and knowledge of safe water sources for drinking. They know which plants could be used as herbs or were good for consumption.

Our group gained valuable insights and knowledge by partnering with these local individuals. Their expertise allowed us to navigate the terrain more efficiently and effectively. We were able to avoid potential risks and hazards making the trek safe, happy, and memorable. Additionally, we learned about the local cultural nuances and their way of life, which added to the overall experience of the trek. The guides made us meet local people. People were very friendly and they welcomed us into their homes. We experienced their warm hospitality in cold mountainous terrain.

Ajay Rawat

Leverage

In the modern world where everything is connected, it's crucial to harness the potential of other individuals and resources to succeed.

With numerous distractions and obstacles, staying focused on your objectives is challenging. You are not able to utilize your strengths efficiently. One key aspect of achieving success is the capacity to utilize the abilities and resources of others. By accessing the skills and expertise of other people, you can enhance your strengths and accomplish your objectives with efficiency and effectiveness. This enables you to achieve impossible dreams. Dreams that may appear to be beyond your capabilities.

The concept of leverage is not new. It has been there throughout history in various forms. We can find references to early philosophies and ancient cultures.

> *"Give me a lever long enough and a fulcrum on which to place it, and I shall move the world."*
> *- Archimedes*

Empty Your Bags. Unlock Your Potential.

This famous quote is from a prominent philosopher, mathematician, and engineer, Archimedes. He was a genius innovator too, who understood the power of leverage and used it to create remarkable marvels.

One of Archimedes' most famous discoveries was the principle of leverage, which he described in his work "On the Equilibrium of Planes." He demonstrated that with a small amount of force applied to a lever, a much larger force could be generated at the other end He also showed that we can increase or decrease the amount of force applied by changing the distance between the force and the fulcrum (the pivot point of the lever).

Archimedes used this principle to design many ingenious devices, including the Archimedes screw (a machine for lifting water), and the Claw of Archimedes (a weapon used to defend against naval attacks).

Archimedes' understanding of leverage had a profound impact on the development of engineering and technology. His work on the principles of mechanics paved the way for the invention of the steam engine, which revolutionized transportation and industry. It also laid the foundation for the development of modern machines. Most machines use levers and other mechanical systems to generate force and perform tasks.

Archimedes left a lasting impact on human civilization through his contributions to the concept of leverage. He provided valuable insights into the mechanics of levers and applied these principles practically, enabling us to use leverage to achieve remarkable feats in engineering and technology. Moreover, this concept can be applied to pursue aspirations or goals beyond an individual's capacity.

Wu-wei

Let us look at the profound concept of Wu Wei, drawing inspiration from Lao Tzu's teachings in the "Tao Te Ching." Wu Wei, often translated as "effortless action" or "non-doing," is a concept that carries deep wisdom. In the given context, I relate it to the practical idea of leverage, as it can transform, the way we approach success and fulfillment in our lives.

Lao Tzu's philosophy is simple yet incredibly powerful. It suggests that a wise leader or individual can attain their goals not by exerting excessive effort or force but by harnessing the resources and talents of those around them. It is where the concept of leverage comes into play.

The essence of Wu Wei is that it invites us to step away from the belief that success can only be achieved through relentless personal effort and control. Instead, it encourages us to create conditions for success, much like a wise leader who focuses on enabling rather than dominating.

To put Wu Wei into practice, we must cultivate an environment of harmony and balance. By creating such a space, we allow everyone to contribute their unique talents and abilities to the common goal. This approach is about humility and selflessness; it's about placing the group's needs ahead of personal desires and ego.

In this way, Lao Tzu's idea of leverage underscores the transformative power of collaboration and teamwork.

Instead of attempting to accomplish everything single-handedly, the wise leader harnesses the resources and talents of those around them to attain success with ease and little resistance. This approach is about recognizing the strengths and potentials of each team member and facilitating their contributions.

By adopting this perspective, you not only reduce the burden of solitary effort but also inspire trust, loyalty, and a strong sense of shared purpose within your team. Wu Wei, in its essence, becomes a reminder that our own success is intricately linked to the success of others. Or, helping others succeed in their goals helps in our own success.

Lao Tzu's teachings, through the lens of leverage, encourage us to rethink our approach to leadership and personal development. By fostering an environment of trust, collaboration, and shared goals, we can tap into a wealth of collective potential, achieving our objectives with far less struggle and resistance. Wu Wei, when applied effectively, reveals that success can be a harmonious journey, where everyone plays their part, and the results are greater than the sum of individual efforts.

Law of karma

In Indian philosophy, the concept of leverage is present in the idea of karma, which suggests that our actions and intentions have a ripple effect on the world around us. By acting with intention and purpose, individuals can leverage the power of karma to achieve their goals and create a positive impact on the world.

The law of karma is a fundamental concept in Hindu, Buddhist, and Jain philosophies that suggests that our actions have consequences that affect our present and future experiences. Karma is often understood as a force that balances our actions and intentions, rewarding good actions and intentions and punishing bad ones.

The concept of leverage is closely connected to the law of karma in that it suggests that we can use our actions and intentions to create positive outcomes and influence the world around us. By acting with intention and purpose, we can leverage our efforts to create positive change in our own lives and in the lives of others.

For example, if we act with kindness and compassion towards others, we can leverage this positive energy to create more positive relationships and experiences. Conversely, if we act with negativity or hostility, we are likely to create more negative experiences for ourselves and those around us.

Similarly, the law of karma suggests that we can leverage our actions and intentions to create positive outcomes in the world. By acting with intention and purpose, we can create positive ripples that spread outwards and affect the people and circumstances around us.

The first step to leveraging your strengths is to understand what they are. What skills or abilities do you possess that you feel confident in? What comes naturally to you that others might struggle with? Do you excel in communication, problem-solving, creativity, or leadership, for example? Understanding your strengths can help you to identify opportunities to put them to use in a way that will bring you success.

Once you have a clear understanding of your strengths, it's time to put them to work. This means seeking out opportunities where you can use your skills and abilities to make a positive impact. Whether it's through volunteering, taking on leadership roles, or working on projects that align with your skills and interests, it's important to find ways to utilize your strengths and make the most of what you have to offer.

In order to maximize your strengths, it's also important to focus on developing them further. This means taking the time to hone your skills and abilities, whether through training, education, or practice. By continually improving your strengths, you will be able to make an even greater impact in your work and personal life.

Empty Your Bags. Unlock Your Potential.

Another important aspect of leveraging your strengths is to create a supportive environment for yourself. This means surrounding yourself with people who believe in you, support you, and encourage you to reach your full potential. A supportive environment can help you to feel confident in using your strengths, and can also provide you with the resources and guidance you need to make the most of them.

Leveraging your strengths is about making the most of your skills and abilities in order to achieve your goals. By understanding your strengths, seeking out opportunities to use them, developing them further, and creating a supportive environment, you can make the most of what you have to offer and live a life that is both fulfilling and successful.

Ajay Rawat

Leveraging from Others: The Benefits of Building Strong Relationships

In addition to leveraging your own strengths and abilities, one can also leverage the strengths of others in order to achieve your goals. Building strong relationships with others can be a powerful tool. This will maximize your potential and help achieve success efficiently.

One of the main benefits of leveraging others is the ability to access a wider range of skills and expertise. By working with others who have different strengths and abilities, you can complement your own skills and create a more well-rounded and effective team. For example, if you are strong in creative problem-solving but weak in technical skills, you can leverage the expertise of others in your network who have the technical knowledge to help you overcome these limitations.

Another key benefit of leveraging from others is the ability to share the burden of responsibilities and workload. When you are working with others, you can divide tasks and responsibilities in a way that allows everyone to focus on their strengths and minimize their weaknesses. This can help to reduce stress and increase productivity, allowing you to achieve your goals more quickly and effectively.

In addition to these practical benefits, building strong relationships with others can also have a positive impact on your personal and professional development. When you work closely with others, you have the opportunity to learn from their experiences and perspectives to grow both personally and professionally. You can receive mentorship and guidance from others. This can be invaluable to help achieve your goals and reach your full potential.

It requires active effort and a willingness to invest time and energy into building connections with others. But more important is a change in mindset. You need to adopt a more collaborative and inclusive approach to working with others.

One way to build strong relationships is to be a supportive and helpful member of your community. This means being willing to lend a hand when others are in need and being open to helping others when they seek assistance. By building a reputation as a reliable and helpful person, you can attract others to work with you and support you in achieving your goals.

Another way to build strong relationships is to be an active listener. To show genuine interest in the perspectives and opinions of others. By taking the time to understand the perspectives of others, you can build rapport and create a more collaborative and supportive relationship.

It is important to be transparent and honest in your relationships with others. This means being upfront about your goals and what you are hoping to achieve and being willing to engage in open and honest dialogue with others. By being transparent and honest, you can build trust and create a more supportive and productive relationship with others.

Leveraging others is an important aspect of maximizing your strengths and achieving success. By building strong relationships with others, you can access a wider range of skills and expertise, share the burden of responsibilities and workload, and benefit from mentorship and guidance. By being supportive, an active listener, and transparent and honest, you can build strong and supportive relationships that will help you to reach your full potential and achieve your goals.

Don't mistake leverage for delegation

Sometimes people mistake leverage for delegation, but they are not the same. Delegation is like passing on your responsibilities to someone else, almost like throwing a burden off your shoulders. With delegation, you distance yourself from the task and tend to forget about it. If something goes wrong, you blame the other person, but if it succeeds, you quickly take credit for it.

However, if we examine delegation closely, we can sense a certain unwillingness behind it. It usually involves tasks or responsibilities that overwhelm us, and we simply want to get rid of them. We push them onto someone else and hope for the best. In this case, the ownership of the task shifts away from us, and we become disconnected from it.

On the other hand, leverage is quite different. When you leverage something, you still remain responsible for it. The ownership stays with you, and you actively participate in the process. Leverage allows you to make the most of your resources, skills, and connections while maintaining a sense of control. You are not merely passing off the task; instead, you are finding ways to maximize its potential.

Leverage works best when both parties involved are closely connected, not necessarily geographically, but emotionally. It's about building a strong relationship with the people you are leveraging. When you leverage effectively, it becomes an empowering idea. You are not exploiting others; instead, they feel valued and important in the collaboration. This mutual trust and respect strengthen the bond between all parties involved.

In contrast, delegation often leads to a sense of detachment. You become disconnected from the task and lose touch with its progress. When failures occur, you tend to blame the person to whom you delegated the task, as they were the ones in charge. However, with leverage, you are actively engaged and accountable. You are aware of the progress and can take immediate action if needed. By remaining responsible, you can adapt and make adjustments along the way, increasing the chances of success.

Remember, delegation is like putting something out of sight and out of mind. It may provide temporary relief, but it lacks the personal touch and involvement that leverage offers. Leverage allows you to harness the collective power and abilities of those around you while maintaining a strong sense of ownership. It's about working together, utilizing resources efficiently, and achieving greater outcomes.

Leverage is an enrolling idea that strengthens relationships and empowers all parties involved. By embracing leverage and avoiding the pitfalls of delegation, you can unlock your potential and achieve remarkable results.

I want to conclude this section by adding two lines from a Hindi poet Arun Kamal which say:

Empty Your Bags. Unlock Your Potential.

अपना क्या है इस जीवन में सब तो लिया उधार
सारा लोहा उन लोगों का अपनी केवल धार।

Before you register this as a nice or interesting concept, I really invite you to start implementing in your life.

We have many successful individuals who have harnessed the power of leverage to achieve their goals and create lasting impact. Their stories can inspire anyone looking to do the same.

Ajay Rawat

Oprah Winfrey: The Power of Leverage in Media

Oprah Winfrey is one of the most successful media personalities of all time. She rose from poverty and adversity to become a household name, thanks in part to her ability to leverage her strengths and those of others. Oprah leveraged her unique talents and her magnetic personality to build a massive media empire, creating a platform that reached millions of people and allowed her to impact the world in a profound way.

Oprah leveraged her relationships with guests, experts, and other media personalities to bring the best and brightest minds to her show. By doing so, she was able to create a powerful and supportive network that helped her achieve greater success. Her network also allowed her to expand her reach and influence beyond the bounds of her own show, as she leveraged her relationships with others to create a wide range of new ventures and opportunities.

Empty Your Bags. Unlock Your Potential.

Elon Musk: The Power of Leverage in Innovation

Elon Musk, known for innovative and visionary entrepreneurship, has been at the forefront of several major technological breakthroughs, including electric cars, solar energy, and space travel. What sets Elon apart is his ability to leverage his strengths and the strengths of others to achieve his goals.

Elon leverages his technical expertise and his ability to think outside the box to create truly innovative products and services. But he also leverages the strengths of others, working closely with engineers, technicians, and other experts to bring his ideas to life. He knows that success requires more than just brilliant ideas - it requires collaboration and teamwork.

Elon also leverages his relationships with investors, partners, and other key players in his industry to secure the funding and support he needs to bring his ideas to market. By doing so, he has been able to achieve results that would be impossible to attain on his own, and to create a legacy of innovation that will impact the world for generations to come.

Ajay Rawat

Mark Zuckerberg: The Power of Leverage in Social Media

Mark Zuckerberg is the founder and CEO of Facebook, one of the largest and most influential social media platforms in the world. One of the core concepts of Mark Zuckerberg's social media business is to leverage user-generated content. Facebook allows users to create and share content with their friends and family, creating a vast network of user-generated content that is constantly being updated and shared.

This user-generated content is the backbone of Facebook's business model. The more content users create and share, the more valuable Facebook becomes. Mark understood this early on and built Facebook's business model around it.

By leveraging user-generated content, Facebook is able to offer advertisers access to a massive, engaged audience. This has made Facebook one of the most effective advertising platforms in the world, with businesses of all sizes using Facebook to reach new customers and grow their businesses.

Mark's success with Facebook demonstrates the power of leverage in social media. By leveraging user-generated content and the strengths of his team, he was able to create a global phenomenon that has transformed the way we communicate and interact with each other.

Empty Your Bags. Unlock Your Potential.

Richard Branson and the Power of Leverage

Richard Branson, the founder of the Virgin Group, is a prime example of someone who has leveraged the strengths of others to achieve great success. From the very beginning, Branson understood the power of collaboration and support, and he surrounded himself with talented and knowledgeable individuals who could help him to achieve his goals.

For example, when Branson launched Virgin Atlantic Airways in 1984, he leveraged his experience in the music industry and his strong relationships with suppliers and distributors to create a unique and successful airline. By leveraging his existing network and relationships, Branson was able to overcome the challenges and obstacles that often come with starting a new business, and he quickly became a leader in the airline industry.

Branson's success with Virgin Atlantic Airways was just the beginning. Over the years, he has continued to leverage the strengths of others to grow his business and achieve great success. Today, the Virgin Group is a multi-billion-dollar conglomerate with businesses in a wide range of industries, including travel, hospitality, financial services, and more.

Leverage is often thought of as a complicated or inaccessible concept. People may think that it's only for the smart, wealthy, or influential, or that it requires special training or education. But this is not the case. Leverage is actually quite simple, and we've all studied it in science class. The word "leverage" comes from "lever," a simple tool or machine that helps one lift heavy objects with less effort. Humans discovered levers early in the evolution of civilizations and used them to create structures and move things around. For example, the ancient Egyptians used levers to build the pyramids and the ancient Hindu temples in India used stones from far-off places that were transported to the top of hills with the help of levers.

One of my favorite examples of leverage in human evolution is the invention of sail boats. With just a simple cloth hoisted on a pole, sailors were able to leverage the power of wind to speed up water transport at a low cost and with high efficiency. To this day, sail boats still captivate us with their simple yet effective use of leverage.

It's important to remember that you don't have to wait to get trained or educated. It's a simple phenomenon that we can all use, and you may already be using it without realizing it. So be aware of your power and use it to your advantage. Leverage can be applied in many aspects of life, including business, finance, politics, and relationships. By leveraging the strengths of others, you can achieve greater success and happiness. You don't need any special training or education to learn how to leverage. In fact, you may already be using it without realizing it. Be aware of your own power and how you can use it to your advantage. With the proper understanding and application of leverage, you can make the most of your resources and achieve more than you ever thought possible.

Warren Buffett

One of the most successful investors of our times. He's known for his disciplined investment approach and his ability to identify and invest in high-quality companies that have the potential to grow and generate significant returns over the long term. But one of the key elements of his success has been his use of leverage.

Buffett has always been a firm believer in using leverage to his advantage. He has used leverage in a number of different ways throughout his career, from using leverage to purchase stocks to using leverage to purchase entire companies. In the early stages of his career, he used leverage to purchase stocks by taking out margin loans. He would then use the profits from those investments to pay off the loans and make additional investments. Over time, this created a positive feedback loop that allowed him to accumulate significant wealth and achieve financial supremacy.

One of the most famous examples of Buffett using leverage to his advantage is his acquisition of Berkshire Hathaway. In 1965, he purchased a controlling stake in the company and transformed it into a holding company that invested in a diverse portfolio of businesses. Today, Berkshire Hathaway is one of the largest and most profitable companies in the world, and its portfolio includes holdings in some of the world's most successful and well-known brands, including Coca-Cola, American Express, and Wells Fargo.

Buffett's success is a testament to the power of leverage. By combining his strengths, including his disciplined investment approach, his ability to identify high-quality companies, and his use of leverage, he has been able to achieve financial success on a scale that few others have ever matched.

So, what can we learn from Warren Buffett's use of leverage? First and foremost, we can see the importance of having a disciplined investment approach. Buffett has always been focused on investing in high-quality companies that have the potential to grow over the long term. This has allowed him to avoid the pitfalls of short-term investing and to build a portfolio that has generated significant returns over the years.

Second, we can see the importance of being able to identify and invest in high-quality companies. Buffett has always been a master at identifying businesses that have the potential to generate significant returns over the long term. This has allowed him to make investments that have produced significant returns, even as the broader market has fluctuated.

Yes, leverage can also be applied to personal relationships, including marriages. One example of leverage in a relationship is the concept of love languages, which was popularized by Gary Chapman in his book "The Five Love Languages." The love languages are five distinct ways that people give and receive love, including acts of service, physical touch, words of affirmation, quality time, and gifts. By understanding and speaking each other's love languages, couples can leverage their individual strengths and preferences to create a stronger and more fulfilling relationship.

For example, if one partner's love language is acts of service, they might feel loved when their partner does things for them like cooking dinner, doing the dishes, or running errands. If the other partner's love language is physical touch,

they might feel loved through hugs, holding hands, or cuddling. By understanding and utilizing each other's love languages, both partners can feel more loved and fulfilled in the relationship.

Another example of leverage in relationships is through mutual support and collaboration. In a successful relationship, both partners work together to achieve their individual and shared goals, leveraging each other's strengths and supporting each other in areas of weakness. This can help to create a stronger and more resilient relationship, where both partners feel valued and appreciated.

For instance, if one partner is great at organizing and planning, they can leverage that strength by taking the lead in planning family events or vacation trips. Meanwhile, the other partner, who may be more creative and spontaneous, can leverage their strengths by coming up with unique and creative ideas for activities and outings. By working together in this way, the couple can leverage their individual strengths to create a more enjoyable and fulfilling life together.

Leveraging strengths and utilizing each other's preferences can be a powerful tool in creating strong relationships, whether it's in a personal partnership or a professional one. By understanding and utilizing the strengths of those around us, we can achieve greater success, happiness, and fulfillment in all areas of our lives.

Leveraging spirituality through guided meditation or seeking the guidance of a guru is a common practice for many individuals looking to enhance their spiritual growth.

One example of leveraging spirituality through guided meditation is the use of guided meditations to help individuals develop mindfulness and inner peace. Many guided meditations are available that are specifically designed to help individuals focus on the present moment and reduce stress and anxiety. By following the guidance of a meditation teacher or audio recording, individuals can more easily enter into a state of deep relaxation and awareness.

Another example of leveraging spirituality is through the guidance of a spiritual teacher or guru. Many spiritual traditions hold that a spiritual teacher can provide invaluable support and guidance to individuals seeking to deepen their spiritual understanding and connection. This can involve regular meetings or interactions with the teacher, as well as participation in spiritual practices and retreats. By seeking the guidance of a spiritual teacher, individuals can leverage the teacher's wisdom, experience, and support to more effectively pursue their spiritual goals.

In both cases, leveraging spirituality through guided meditation or the guidance of a spiritual teacher can help individuals achieve greater success and fulfillment in their spiritual journey. By seeking out the support and guidance of those who have gone before us, we can leverage their experience and wisdom to more effectively reach our own spiritual goals.

I want to share another story about leverage, which we all might know, but not as an example of power of leverage.

Edmund Hillary and Tenjing Norgay

Two of the most famous names in the world of mountaineering. In 1953, they became the first climbers to reach the summit of Mount Everest, the tallest mountain in the world. But they didn't do it alone. Hillary and Norgay relied heavily on the skills and expertise of a local Sherpa, who acted as their guide and support system throughout their journey.

The Sherpas, who are an ethnic group from the high-altitude regions of Nepal, have a deep understanding of the mountain and the environment in which it exists. They have lived in these regions for generations, and have developed a unique set of skills and knowledge that make them experts in climbing and surviving in the high-altitude environment. Hillary and Norgay leveraged this expertise to their advantage, using the Sherpa's guidance and support to help them reach the summit of Mount Everest.

The Sherpa not only acted as a guide, but also provided essential support in the form of carrying supplies, setting up camps, and helping with navigation. This support allowed Hillary and Norgay to focus on their climbing and minimize the risks they faced. It also allowed them to conserve their energy, as they didn't have to worry about the added weight of supplies and equipment.

Hillary and Norgay's story is a classic example of how leverage can help us achieve great things. By relying on the expertise and support of others, they were able to overcome obstacles and reach their goal. It shows us that leverage isn't just about financial or material gain, but can also be applied in more personal and emotional contexts. In this case, it allowed Hillary and Norgay to achieve a great feat in the world of mountaineering, and inspired countless others to follow in their footsteps.

Story of Edmund Hillary and Tenjing Norgay shows us the power of leverage in achieving great things. By relying on the skills and expertise of others, they were able to overcome obstacles and reach their goal. It serves as a reminder that we can all benefit from leveraging the strengths of others, and that there is often more to be gained from working together than from working alone.

I would like to share a personal example of how I leveraged my resources to achieve a major project. I was presented with the opportunity to work on a corporate film project that required traveling to five different states in India within two months. This seemed like an impossible task considering my day job, family commitments, and training schedules, not to mention I had already booked tickets for a family vacation in the middle of the shoot.

But my passion for the project and the creative fulfillment it promised, made me pause before declining the offer. Instead, I said yes without even thinking about how I would manage it all. After accepting the project, I started to work on the planning and found a partner in a friend who was willing to join me on the project.

Together, we built the team, planned out all the shoot requirements, equipment, and personnel. We sent the team to the various locations and I was able to direct them via phone calls and shared storyboards. It was a stroke of luck that one of the shoot locations was in the same city as my family vacation and on the same dates, saving me money on hiring a crew for those days.

The outcome was even better than we expected and the client was so pleased that they gave us two more projects. Through this experience, I was able to leverage my resources and achieve this large task without having to take a break from my day job, miss my vacation, or skip any of my training.

So, don't be afraid to use leverage in your own life, and be mindful of its potential to help you accomplish your goals.

Empty your time bag using leverage, and see how much more you can accomplish with more speed. This will help you expand your capabilities and accomplish your dreams quickly, making room for more.

This will leave you with a lot more time, to achieve goals faster or take on more goals.

Exercise:
I invite you to take a moment to write down examples of the use of leverage. Given below are two columns: one in which you list 10 instances where you used leverage to cause breakthrough results, and another in which you list instances of using leverage unknowingly.

Empty Your Bags. Unlock Your Potential.

Instance of leverage knowingly	**Instance of leverage unknowingly**
_____	_____
_____	_____
_____	_____
_____	_____
_____	_____

Ajay Rawat

Empty Your Bag Of Heart

Inspire to involve

Empty Your Bags. Unlock Your Potential.

Building relationships for a successful pursuit

After spending five days trekking, we were on our way back to our campsite, close to the only motorable road in the valley. Throughout the trek, we faced numerous challenges, especially during the three days when we were at an altitude of more than 4000 meters. The scenic beauty of the place was awe-inspiring. We had overcome all hardships, which had now turned into cherished memories. Despite all that, we were a little disappointed. Few of us expected to see some snow on our trek, but we did not come across any during the entire trek. We could see some snow on higher peaks. Those peaks were at a good distance and did not fall in our route.

During the trek, I became friends with a person, I had met for the first time. We had hardly spoken while climbing up as I was trailing at the end of the group, and while coming back, I had picked up some speed. Throughout the trek, I took numerous pictures. It was our common interest, and we bonded well during the return. We both shared a common interest in photography.

We both shared the keen desire to see some snow up close, but everyone else, including the local guides, was too exhausted to help us. After a lot of insistence and requests, the guides finally revealed that there was a glacier patch close to our trekking route, but it was a major detour. Nobody in the group was willing to take that detour.

Fortunately, my new friend and I quickly enrolled ourselves in the idea, and within a minute or so, we were on our way to the glacier. There was no need for extensive conversations or negotiations, but a simple sense of agreement. We climbed a tiring path, crossing big boulders and streams. Both of us were a bit unsure and doubted our decision to move away from the group and come on this uncharted trail. But it was all worth it. After an hour, we finally reached a massive cave formed in the glacier. That was an unforgettable and breathtaking experience. It was like icing on the cake of our entire trek.

Had we not enrolled the local guides and ourselves in the idea of exploring the glacier patch, our desire would have remained unfulfilled. I am glad that the enrolment with my photo friend made the trip even more memorable. It was exciting that two of us got to experience something unique from the rest of the group.

Partnerships and alliances

It is imperative to have a growth and expansion mindset for personal and professional development. Stagnancy or being at status quo is synonymous with shrinking. Everything around us is in a constant state of change and growth. So, if we are not moving ahead, we are actually drifting behind. If you want to move forward, it is important to take charge of the situation and switch gears towards progress.

The idea of reducing possessions and expanding simultaneously may seem contradictory, but it is possible to expand and grow without accumulating more resources.

One's own capacity and resources are not the only factors that determine the possibility of expansion. In fact, real expansion happens only when one moves beyond one's capacity. Innovation and creativity can help individuals think beyond their limitations and explore new ideas for growth and development. Sometimes, it's not about acquiring more resources, but rather utilizing the existing resources effectively or finding innovative solutions to problems that limit our progress. For example, instead of investing in expensive tools or technology, one can leverage the power of social media and online platforms to reach a wider audience or customer base. This approach not only saves money but also creates new opportunities for growth and expansion. Therefore, thinking outside of one's own capacity and resources is key to achieving expansion and success in both personal and professional domains.

We can always explore new and innovative ways of working. We must consider the power of alliances, partnerships, and forming groups. These can provide the necessary support and resources to achieve expansion goals that may be appear beyond our limitations. Working together with like-minded individuals who share our vision not only bring fresh ideas and perspectives but also create a strong support network that helps us achieve our goals more efficiently.

Partnerships and alliances can come in many forms. It can be collaborating with a friend or joining a community organization. The important thing is to find like-minded individuals with complementary strengths and skills who can help achieve a common goal. Collaborations allow for a division of tasks, sharing of resources, and tapping into each other's networks. It can lead to exponential growth and success. Group efforts can foster a sense of community, accountability, and motivation. They provide an opportunity to learn from others, share experiences, and gain new insights. By working together, individuals can overcome obstacles and challenges that may arise during their expansion journey. Therefore, building partnerships and alliances is an effective way to achieve personal and professional growth, regardless of the specific context or industry.

Empty Your Bags. Unlock Your Potential.

Working in a group can create a sense of belonging and a shared sense of purpose, leading to a feeling of community. This community aspect can be crucial for overcoming obstacles and challenges that may arise in the pursuit of growth and expansion. When individuals work together, they can offer each other support and guidance. It helps to keep everyone motivated and accountable. In addition, when one person is struggles, others can help, creating a safety net that can make taking risks and pursuing ambitious goals less daunting.

Collaboration can also provide an opportunity for individuals to learn from others, share experiences, and gain new insights. When working in a group, individuals can bring their own unique perspectives and experiences to the table, which can help to spur innovation and creativity. By hearing different points of view, individuals can expand their own understanding and consider new ideas. In this way, group efforts can lead to growth and expansion on both an individual and collective level.

These benefits are not limited to business or professional pursuits. Group efforts are evident in team sports, artistic collaborations, and personal growth journeys. Working together towards a shared goal can help individuals develop deeper connections with others and achieve things they may not have been able to achieve alone.

Ajay Rawat

Power of communication

To ask someone to agree, support, or replace them, one can use various approaches that fall under different categories of communication. These categories include convincing, influencing, directing, threatening, punishing, motivating, manipulating, and enrolment. All these approaches come under the broad umbrella of communication, which can be verbal or non-verbal. However, it is crucial to be mindful of our communication and the power of our words. The way we communicate can either strengthen or weaken our relationships, and we always have a choice in how we choose to communicate.

Effective communication can make a significant difference in how we interact with others. It is essential to be mindful of the words we use. What language do we use when we approach a situation? Using positive and genuine language can create strong bonds with others and gain their trust and support. On the other hand, negative or manipulative language can destroy relationships and lead to mistrust and resentment. Ultimately, our choice of communication approach can have a significant impact on the outcome of the situation.

Let us look at how these ways of communicating are different from each other. How effectively they work.

Convincing someone involves presenting logical arguments, facts, and evidence to persuade them to see things from your perspective. It's a process of presenting a strong case that can influence the other person's decision-making process. However, it can be challenging to convince someone who has different values and beliefs deeply ingrained than your own.

Influencing someone involves appealing to their emotions and values to create an emotional connection with them. The goal is to sway them towards a certain action or decision. For example, a celebrity endorsing a product can influence people to buy it.

Directing someone involves telling them what to do in a straightforward manner. It can be effective when the person being directed is in a position to take orders, such as in a work setting. However, it can also come across as bossy or authoritarian if not executed correctly.

Threatening someone involves using fear to motivate them to take a certain action. For example, a parent threatens to ground their child if they don't do their homework. However, this approach can backfire if the person being threatened feels intimidated or resentful.

Punishing someone involves imposing negative consequences if they don't comply with your requests. For example, an employer firing an employee for not meeting their performance targets. This approach can be effective in some cases, but can also create resentment and a negative work environment.

Motivating someone involves inspiring them to take action by appealing to their interests, desires, and aspirations. For example, a coach motivates their team to work hard by reminding them of their shared goals. This approach works when people are intrinsically motivated, not when they lack motivation.

Manipulating someone involves using deception or underhanded tactics to achieve your desired outcome. This approach is unethical and can damage relationships.

Enrolling someone involves inviting them to contribute to your goals and vision. It's a collaborative approach that creates a sense of shared ownership and commitment. Enrolment is about building trust, establishing a connection, and presenting a compelling vision that resonates with the other person. This approach is effective in building strong relationships and achieving common goals.

There is no definitive way or the best approach, which depends on the situation and the individuals involved. In some cases, directing or motivating may be the most appropriate approach, while enrolment may be more effective for others.

Saam, daam, dand, bhed

Four guiding principles of diplomacy in ancient Indian philosophy. These four strategies, which translate to conciliation, reward, punishment, and division, respectively, are believed to be effective methods for bringing people together and maintaining peace in society. Each of these principles is based on a different approach to resolving differences and can be applied in various situations depending on the nature of the situation. Although these principles are ancient, their relevance and significance in modern-day diplomacy are still widely recognized. In this article, we will explore each of the four guiding principles and how they can be used to promote harmony and cooperation among people.

Saam, also known as Sam or Saman, is a Sanskrit term that refers to the art of conciliation or persuasion through discussion and negotiation. It involves seeking a solution that is acceptable to all parties involved by finding common ground and mutual benefits. The Saam approach is rooted in the idea that a peaceful and harmonious resolution to a conflict can be achieved through respectful dialogue and understanding. This approach emphasizes the importance of active listening, empathy, and diplomacy in building relationships and resolving disputes.

In practice, Saam involves creating an environment of trust and respect, where all parties feel heard and understood. The Saam approach encourages individuals to approach negotiations with an open mind and a willingness to find common ground. It recognizes that every party has its own interests and needs and seeks to find a solution that meets those needs while also satisfying the needs of others.

Saam is often used in situations where parties have a long-standing relationship or ongoing interaction, such as in business partnerships or family relationships. It is also used in political and international diplomacy where negotiations require delicate handling to maintain positive relationships between countries or groups. By focusing on finding common ground and working towards a mutually beneficial solution, Saam can be an effective tool for building lasting relationships and resolving conflicts peacefully.

Daam, also known as Daman or Dana, is a Sanskrit term that refers to the approach of incentivizing or offering rewards to gain cooperation and achieve desired outcomes. This approach is based on the idea that people can be motivated by material or monetary gain, and that by providing incentives, individuals can be influenced to take certain actions or make specific decisions.

In practice, Daam involves identifying what motivates the other party and offering an incentive that aligns with their interests. This approach can be effective in situations where the other party is motivated by self-interest and can be swayed by material or monetary gain. For example, in business negotiations, a company may offer a discount or bonus to a supplier in exchange for a larger order or faster delivery. Similarly, in politics, politicians may offer specific policies or benefits to gain the support of specific groups or voters.

However, Daam can also have negative connotations, as it can be perceived as bribery or unethical behavior. Therefore, it is important to ensure that the incentives offered are legal and ethical and do not cross any ethical or legal boundaries. Additionally, Daam may not be effective in situations where the other party's motivations are based on factors other than self-interest, such as morality or principles.

Dand, also known as Danda or Dandaniti, is a Sanskrit term that refers to the approach of using punishment or force to achieve compliance. This approach is based on the idea that individuals can be motivated by the fear of consequences, and that by using threats or force, individuals can be coerced into taking certain actions or making specific decisions.

In practice, Dand involves identifying consequences for non-compliance and communicating those consequences to the other party. This approach can be effective in situations where the other party is resistant to persuasion or motivated by the fear of consequences. For example, a government may threaten to impose economic sanctions on another country if it does not comply with certain demands.

The use of Dand or punishment can cause significant damage to interpersonal relationships, often in ways that may not be immediately visible. In contrast to open conflict or aggression, the use of punishment can create an atmosphere of fear and mistrust, leading to resentment and a breakdown of communication. This can be particularly damaging in personal relationships, where the repercussions of using punishment can be silent but long-lasting. The use of force or punishment can be perceived as aggressive or unethical, and may even escalate the conflict, making it more difficult to achieve a peaceful resolution. Therefore, it is important to carefully consider the potential impact of using the Dand approach, and to explore alternative options that prioritize constructive communication and understanding in interpersonal relationships.

Bhed, also known as "divide and rule," is an approach that involves creating divisions or sowing seeds of doubt among opponents in order to gain an advantage. This strategy has been used throughout history, often by those in positions of power, to maintain control over their subjects.

One example of the use of Bhed can be seen in the British colonization of India. The British East India Company, which controlled much of India in the 18th and 19th centuries, employed a strategy of divide and rule to maintain their power. They exploited existing divisions between different ethnic and religious groups, pitting them against each other and sowing seeds of doubt and mistrust. For example, the British encouraged tensions between Hindus and Muslims, which eventually led to the partition of India in 1947.

While the Bhed approach can be effective in situations where opponents are already divided or weakened, it can also lead to further polarization and conflict. It can create lasting divisions between groups and erode trust, making it more difficult to achieve peace and reconciliation. In many cases, the use of Bhed has been seen as an unethical and manipulative tactic that serves only the interests of those in power.

The division of Germany into East and West after World War II is another example of the Bhed approach. After the war, Germany was divided into two separate states: The Federal Republic of Germany (West Germany) and the German Democratic Republic (East Germany). The division was the result of political differences between the Western Allies and the Soviet Union, which occupied Eastern Germany.

In order to maintain control over the East German population, the Communist government employed a strategy of divide and rule. They exploited existing divisions between different groups, such as workers and intellectuals, in order to weaken opposition to their rule. They also created a network of informants, who reported on dissenters and helped to suppress opposition.

Meanwhile, in West Germany, the government worked to rebuild the country's economy and establish democracy. The two Germanys developed along very different paths, with different political systems, economies, and cultures.

The division between East and West Germany lasted for more than 40 years, until the fall of the Berlin Wall in 1989 and the reunification of Germany in 1990. While the Bhed approach was effective in maintaining control over the East German population, it also created lasting divisions between the two halves of the country. The reunification process was difficult and required a great deal of effort to overcome the mistrust and animosity that had developed over the years.

Empty Your Bags. Unlock Your Potential.

Inspiring to involve

Out of the four the Saam approach to conflict resolution has stood the test of time because it prioritizes peaceful and respectful dialogue over force and manipulation. Ancient Indian gurus taught their students, including kings, princes, and noblemen, that conciliation and negotiation were essential for building strong relationships and political alliances. They understood that punishment and manipulation could create more problems than they solved, and so they emphasized the importance of finding common ground and mutual benefits.

Inspiring to involve, as an approach to building relationships, is a prime example of the Saam approach in action. Rather than trying to convince or manipulate people to do what you want, enrolment is about inviting others to contribute to your goals and vision. It involves active listening, empathy, and diplomacy, and it seeks to find solutions that are acceptable to all parties involved. By using enrolment as a way to build relationships, educators can create a sense of community that is supportive and inclusive. This may sound like 'influence' to some people, and I would say both terms are close but yet distinct. Influence involves using tactics and techniques to shape or change someone's thoughts or actions. It relies on persuasion, manipulation, and the use of social proof or authority.

Robert Cialdini, a renowned psychologist, wrote a popular book called "Influence: The Psychology of Persuasion," which delves into the principles and techniques of influence. In the book, Cialdini outlines six key principles that play a significant role in influencing others: reciprocity, commitment and consistency, social proof, authority, liking, and scarcity. These principles shed light on how people can be swayed or persuaded in various situations, whether in marketing, sales, or personal interactions.

The art of persuasion, as described by Cialdini, involves using these principles strategically to influence others' decisions or actions. It focuses on understanding human psychology and employing tactics that appeal to people's emotions, beliefs, and desires. Persuasion can be a powerful tool when used ethically and responsibly, but it can also be manipulative if employed solely for personal gain or to deceive others.

There is one more word I would to distinguish from 'Inspire to involve', that is, motivation. Again, it appears to be very close but yet not the same. What is motivation? As per dictionary, motivation means 'the act or an instance of motivating, or providing with a reason to act in a certain way'. Or simply put, motivation is a reason or reasons for acting or behaving in a particular way.

There is some great work done by two psychologists studying about motivation. Edward Deci and Richard Ryan, psychologists who conducted research on motivation, explored different types of motivation and developed the self-determination theory. Their theory highlights the importance of the quality or regulation of motivation. They identified intrinsic motivation, extrinsic motivation, and amotivation as primary categories. As per Deci and Ryan Intrinsic motivation arises from internal desires, enjoyment, or satisfaction derived from engaging in an activity for its own sake. Extrinsic motivation, on the other hand, stems from external factors such as rewards, punishments, or recognition. Amotivation reflects a lack of motivation or a perception that a task is irrelevant or unattainable.

On the contrary, the Saam approach and enrolment prioritize building relationships based on mutual respect and understanding. This can lead to stronger and more lasting relationships that benefit everyone involved.

Inspiring to involve or if we can call it Enrolment is a much stronger approach than convincing or manipulating people to do what you want. When you enroll others, you are inviting them to be a part of something bigger than themselves, to contribute their unique skills, talents, and perspectives to a shared vision. In this way, enrolment is not about getting people to do what you want, but rather about building a shared understanding and commitment to a common goal. This approach is much more sustainable in the long run, as it builds trust and buy-in from others, rather than simply imposing your will on them.

In order to build successful relationships through enrolment, there are certain key elements that are necessary. One of the most critical of these is genuine-ness. People can quickly sense when someone is not being truthful or authentic, and this can quickly erode trust and make it difficult to enroll others in your vision or goals. On the other hand, when your words and actions are aligned, and you are truly invested in your message, others will be much more likely to believe in what you are saying and be willing to support you.

Genuine-ness requires that you are honest with yourself and with others about your intentions, values, and goals. When you are clear about what you stand for and what you want to achieve, it becomes much easier to communicate your message in a way that is authentic and compelling. This means that you need to take the time to reflect on your own values and goals, and to ensure that they align with your actions and words.

Inspiring to involve or Enrolment is a powerful tool for building strong relationships, but it must be genuine and sincere to be effective. If you are faking your enthusiasm or trying to manipulate others, it will not be true enrolment. People are able to sense when someone is not being authentic, and this can quickly impact trust and damage relationships. For example, when a salesperson lists out all the benefits of a product, but the customer can sense that the salesperson is only interested in making a sale, it can be off-putting and reduce the chances of a successful sale.

Empty Your Bags. Unlock Your Potential.

The importance of genuine enrolment can also be seen in social situations. Women, in particular, are often approached by men who are not truly interested in getting to know them, but are instead focused on their own desires. This kind of approach is rarely successful and can even be harmful to both parties. In short, it is important to approach enrolment with sincerity and authenticity, rather than trying to manipulate or deceive others.

The human heart is the seat of emotions, passions, and desires. When we approach others with a clear heart, we are able to connect with them on a deeper level and inspire them to take action towards a shared vision or goal. In this context, a clear heart refers to a heart that is emptied of any resistance, preconceived notions, biases, or resentment. It is a heart that is free from fear or inhibitions and allows others to see the authentic human being behind the invitation. In this essay, we will explore the importance of having a clear heart when inspiring others to get involved in our own dreams and goals.

To begin with, having a clear heart is crucial when it comes to building trust with others. Trust is the foundation of any successful relationship, and it is particularly important when it comes to inspiring others to take action towards a shared goal. When we approach others with a heart that is free from any preconceived notions or biases, we create an environment of openness and acceptance. This allows others to feel safe and to trust that we have their best interests at heart. When we are able to build this kind of trust, it becomes much easier to inspire others to get involved in our own dreams and goals.

Another reason why having a clear heart is important is that it allows us to be more present and attentive to the needs of others. When we are free from resentment or other negative emotions, we are able to focus more fully on the present moment and on the people around us. This allows us to listen more deeply to the concerns and ideas of others, and to be more responsive to their needs. When we are able to show this kind of attentiveness and care, others are much more likely to feel inspired and motivated to join us in our pursuit.

In addition to building trust and being present with others, having a clear heart also allows us to be more vulnerable and authentic in our interactions. When we are free from fear or inhibitions, we are able to be more honest and transparent about our own struggles and challenges. This kind of vulnerability can be incredibly powerful in inspiring others to get involved in our own dreams and goals. When we are able to show others that we are not perfect, and that we too face challenges and obstacles, it can make our own pursuits seem more accessible and relatable.

Therefore, having a clear heart also allows us to be more creative and innovative in our approach. When we are free from any preconceived notions or biases, we are able to approach problems and challenges with fresh eyes and an open mind. This kind of creative thinking can be incredibly valuable when it comes to inspiring others to get involved in our own dreams and goals. When we are able to come up with innovative solutions and ideas, others are much more likely to see the potential and possibility in our pursuits.

A clear heart allows us to create a sense of shared purpose and meaning with others. When we approach others with a heart that is free from any resentment or negative emotions, we are able to create an environment of positivity and optimism. This kind of positive energy can be incredibly infectious, and can inspire others to see the potential and possibility in our own dreams and goals. When we are able to create a sense of shared purpose and meaning, others are much more likely to feel invested in our pursuit and to take action towards a shared vision.

Another key element of successful enrolment is emotional energy. When you are passionate and enthusiastic about your vision, it becomes contagious, and others will be much more likely to want to be a part of it. This means that you need to find ways to tap into your own passion and energy, and to communicate it in a way that is infectious.

One way to do this is to focus on the positive impact that your vision will have on others. When people can see how your goals and vision align with their own values and aspirations, they are much more likely to be motivated to support you. This requires that you take the time to listen to others and understand their needs and desires, and to frame your message in a way that resonates with them. Whether you are working to enroll others in your goals or building relationships with friends and family, it takes time, effort, and energy to establish and maintain strong connections.

Another way to generate emotional energy is to create a sense of urgency around your vision. It means there is a limited or finite time to accomplish the goal. When people feel that there is a pressing need to act, they are much more likely to be motivated to support your goals. This requires that you are clear about the potential consequences of inaction, and that you communicate this in a way that is compelling and urgent.

Enrolment is not just about communicating your message effectively; it also requires that you listen to others and understand their perspectives. This means that you need to be open to feedback and willing to adapt your approach based on the input of others. When you are able to demonstrate that you value the input of others and are willing to incorporate their feedback into your vision, it builds trust and strengthens your relationship.

Enrolment requires that you are patient and persistent. Building strong relationships takes time, and it may require multiple conversations and interactions before you are able to enroll others in your vision. This means that you need to be willing to invest the time and effort required to build trust and establish a shared commitment to your goals.

Empty Your Bags. Unlock Your Potential.

Often people think about applying force as an obvious choice to get the desired output, especially when you have the power. Despite that force and coercion often fail to deliver the desired results. This was perfectly illustrated by the famous image of a Chinese protestor standing peacefully in front of ten military tanks during the Tiananmen Square protests in 1989. The image captured the world's attention and became a powerful symbol of the power of peaceful resistance and the futility of force.

The protestor's bravery in the face of overwhelming force serves as a powerful reminder of the limits of coercion and the importance of enrolling others through genuine and heartfelt communication. In this context, the enrolment becomes a key aspect in the pursuit of success and fulfillment, and it's a powerful tool for bringing people together in support of a common goal.

In order to effectively enroll others, it's important to understand their motivations, values, and desires. By understanding what drives others, you can craft a message that resonates with them and speaks directly to their needs and aspirations. This helps to build trust and establish a connection that can be leveraged to create a strong and supportive relationship.

Ajay Rawat

Building relationships with authenticity

Inspiring to involve others in your goals and ambitions requires a deep sense of purpose, clarity, and confidence. When you are clear about what you want to achieve, and you have a strong sense of purpose, others will be more likely to be enrolled in your vision. Confidence and self-assuredness are also critical, as they signal to others that you believe in what you are doing and are capable of achieving your goals.

Enrolment is a powerful tool for building relationships and achieving your goals. Here are some key points to keep in mind when using effective communication for enrolment:

Be genuine and authentic: People can easily sense when someone is being insincere or dishonest. Make sure your words and actions align with your true intentions and beliefs.

Pay attention to what others are saying: Effective communication is more than just speaking; it's also about understanding. When you actively listen, you demonstrate that you appreciate the perspective of the speaker and are open-minded to novel concepts.

Use positive language: Positive language can help create a welcoming and supportive environment. Use words and phrases that convey enthusiasm, optimism, and inclusivity.

Use storytelling: Stories can be a powerful tool for enrolment. They can help illustrate your vision and create an emotional connection with your audience.

Find common ground: Look for shared values, goals, or interests that you can use as a basis for your enrolment efforts. When you find common ground, it can help build trust and create a sense of collaboration.

Offer something of value: To enroll others, it's important to offer something of value. This could be an opportunity to learn, grow, or contribute to a worthwhile cause.

Be persistent: Enrolling others is not always easy, and it often requires persistence and patience. Don't give up too quickly, and be willing to adapt your approach as needed.

By keeping these points in mind and using effective communication techniques, you can become a more effective enroller and build stronger relationships with others.

Enrolment is not solely dependent on one's communication skills or ability to articulate their message effectively. While these factors can certainly help in the enrolment process, there are other elements at play that can make a person influential and successful in enrolling others in their vision or goals.

Take the example of Mahatma Gandhi, who was not considered to be the most eloquent or polished speaker, yet he had millions of followers who embraced his principles and philosophy. What made him successful in enrolling so many people in his vision was his unwavering commitment to his message, his authenticity and integrity, and his ability to connect with people on a deep emotional level.

Gandhi's principles of non-violent resistance, civil disobedience, and communal harmony resonated deeply with people who were seeking freedom and justice in colonial India. His unwavering commitment to these principles, even in the face of immense opposition and persecution, earned him the trust and respect of millions of people across the country.

Gandhi's authenticity and integrity were also critical to his success in enrolling others in his vision. He lived a simple and austere life, eschewing material wealth and power, and was known for his unwavering moral and ethical compass. His actions were always aligned with his words, and people trusted him implicitly because of this.

Gandhi's ability to connect with people on a deep emotional level was also a key factor in his success as a leader. He was able to tap into the hopes and fears of his followers, and his message resonated deeply with them on a spiritual and emotional level. His willingness to listen to people's concerns and empathize with their struggles helped him build strong relationships with his followers, and this in turn made him much more effective in enrolling them in his vision.

Strong communication skills and good articulation can certainly help in the enrolment process, there are other factors at play that can make a person successful in enrolling others in their vision or goals. Mahatma Gandhi's example teaches us that authenticity, integrity, unwavering commitment to one's message, and the ability to connect with people on a deep emotional level are also critical to success in enrolling others.

Enrollment is more than just persuading others to join your vision or goals. It involves inspiring and being open-minded to new ideas and opportunities. When you are open to new ideas, you create a learning environment that fosters growth and can lead to unexpected insights.

Open-mindedness also means being receptive to feedback and constructive criticism. By considering different perspectives, you can refine your goals and develop a stronger message that resonates with others. Incorporating feedback helps you create a compelling vision that inspires support.

Moreover, being open-minded helps you build a supportive network. When you embrace different perspectives, you attract like-minded individuals who share your values and goals. By nurturing these relationships, you create a community that can support you in achieving your goals.

The power of enrollment lies in its magnetic effect. When you are genuinely invested in your vision, others can sense it, and they are more likely to be drawn towards it. Trust, authenticity, and genuine-ness are the foundation of this magnetic effect. It not only influences individuals but also has the potential to impact groups and organizations.

Enrollment is an art that plays a crucial role in building relationships and pursuing ambitious goals. By understanding key elements like genuine-ness, emotional energy, effective communication, clarity, purpose, and open-mindedness, you can establish a supportive network that helps you achieve your ambitions.

Talking about authencity, I've seen some amazing moments where people instantly connect, be it one-on-one or in larger groups. I've experienced this myself, making breakthroughs in tough times. This got me curious, and I decided to dig deeper into it. I want to unravel the magic of authenticity in human relationships, trust, and inspiration. Let's explore its impact and understand how it inspires people not only to get your vision but to actively be part of making it real.

Authenticity is like the spark that makes these magical connections happen. It's being genuinely yourself, without any masks, and it resonates strongly with others. These connections aren't just quick moments; they're the foundation of trust and meaningful relationships.

Authenticity isn't just about talking about a vision; it's about living it genuinely. This honesty is magnetic, going beyond words to create a feeling. People don't just get the communication; they feel the authenticity behind it, making them want to actively contribute to making it happen.

Authenticity is the key to real connection and getting inspired to involve themselves. The magic is in being open, making a space where people feel seen and heard. It's not just a personal thing; it's a force that goes beyond one person, shaping shared goals and purposes.

As we unwrap this magic, let it be an invitation to embrace authenticity not just as an idea but as a guide. By doing so, we open up to making connections that go beyond the surface, building trust and sparking involvement in the hearts of those who share our vision and purpose. This journey into authenticity isn't just about getting it; it's about experiencing the power in each real connection.

We have discovered authenticity as a magical potion that transforms ordinary relationships into something extraordinary. That's the alchemy of authenticity. It's about being genuinely yourself, without hiding behind masks or pretending to be someone you're not. This genuine expression creates a special connection that goes deeper than just talking; it's like having a secret key that opens the door to trust. Making authenticity the very foundation of any meaningful relationship.

Authenticity is the art of showing the world your true colors. It's like saying, "This is who I am, no filters, no disguises." When we let our true selves shine, unburdened by the need to impress or conform, it creates a space for something remarkable to happen. It's not just about saying the right words; it's about embodying the values and beliefs that define us.

That makes authenticity a guiding light. Not just illuminating your vision but inviting others to actively join in its realization. The magic lies in authenticity resonating on a deep, instinctive level. It's more than conveying a vision; it's authentically living it. This authenticity possesses a magnetic quality – individuals don't just observe your vision; they emotionally connect with it. This emotional connection motivates action.

Authenticity becomes a dynamic force, inviting participation instead of passive observation. It's not just about understanding the vision; it's about feeling the authenticity behind it. This feeling becomes the spark that ignites action, turning individuals from spectators into active contributors. In the realm of inspiration and involvement, authenticity is the catalyst propelling visions from concepts to living, breathing realities.

Recent breakthroughs in neuroscience provide a fascinating lens through which we can understand the impact of authenticity on human connection. Authenticity, it turns out, is a neural load reducer. When we are authentic, our brains operate with more efficiency, unburdened by the cognitive gymnastics of managing inconsistencies.

In 2009 Journal of Neuroscience published a study. University of Southern California's researchers investigated the influence of authentic interactions on neural activities. Cognitive dissonance is a state of discomfort arising from conflicting beliefs or behaviors. An example of Cognitive dissonance is when someone believes that smoking is unhealthy yet continues to smoke.

The study involved 32 participants divided into two groups authentic and superficial interaction groups. Studies revealed that authentic exchanges led to decreased amygdala activity. We have learned about the amygdala which is responsible for processing emotions such as fear. This reduction in neural activity in the amygdala was linked to a simultaneous increase in the ventromedial prefrontal cortex (VMPFC), associated with empathy and social cognition.

The researchers proposed that authentic interactions contribute to reducing feelings of uncertainty and threat. That has a positive influence on our mental and emotional health.

During the study, the group of participants engaged in authentic interactions shared personally meaningful experiences. On the other hand, superficial interaction groups focused on neutral topics. The team used functional magnetic resonance imaging (fMRI) to study brain activities. The data revealed reduced amygdala activity and increased VMPFC activity in the authentic interaction group.

If you look at it, the implications of this research are profound. The results suggest that authentic interactions mitigate cognitive dissonance and foster empathy. It also brought positive effects on mental and emotional well-being. Inconsistencies in values or exposure to conflicting information can trigger Cognitive dissonance. That can be addressed by modifying beliefs or behaviors, rationalizing conflicts, or avoiding triggering situations.

Overall, this study supports the cultivation of authentic interactions in our lives. Recognizing our potential to enhance connections, alleviate stress, and foster a sense of ease.

Think about the most authentic conversations you've had. They weren't just exchanges of information; they were shared moments where both parties were fully present. Authenticity, therefore, becomes a catalyst for deep, meaningful connections rooted in the richness of the present.

Presence in the Now: Authenticity has way more benefits, which goes beyond cognitive benefits. It acts as a gateway to a profound sense of presence in the present moment. Being in "now". When we shed the burden of upholding facades and navigating inconsistencies, we open ourselves to fully engage in the "now." This is referred to as the heightened state of living. This heightened state of presence possesses a magical magnetic quality. It draws others into the current moment and establishes connections that transcend the limitations of time.

Consider the most authentic conversations you've experienced. You would have realized that they weren't mere exchanges of information; they were shared moments where both parties were wholly present. Authenticity serves as a catalyst. It propels individuals into a space where connections go beyond what is communicated. It is rooted in the depth and richness of the present.

In the hustle of daily life, authentic moments become like beacons in the fog, cutting through distractions and inviting individuals to connect on a more meaningful level. When authenticity guides interactions, there is a shared acknowledgment of the present moment's significance. Creating an environment where genuine connections can flourish.

The magnetic pull of authenticity in the present is akin to a shared journey. Like a dance where both participants synchronize their steps in the rhythm of the moment. It's not merely about the words spoken but the shared experience of being fully present, creating a resonance that lingers beyond the conversation.

Talking about Resonance, it is a different realm of conversation with frequencies and wavelengths. There is a whole new world to be discovered for resonance in the context of human connections and relationships. They are important in establishing spiritual connections too. Where the intricate dance of these cosmic vibrations has a profound significance, particularly in causing spiritual connections. Within this paradigm, there exists a compelling school of thought suggesting that these frequencies are the threads that weave the fabric of the universe, connecting every element in a grand tapestry of existence. We will discuss this phenomenon later sometime but let's come back to authenticity.

Another interesting characteristic of Authenticity is that it is contagious. When one person embodies authenticity, it encourages a reciprocal response from others. That creates a ripple effect that extends beyond individual interactions. Authenticity becomes a shared commitment to embrace the richness of the present, fostering a collective consciousness that values each moment as a unique and irreplaceable gift.

In essence, authenticity's role in facilitating a heightened presence in the now is pivotal. It transforms conversations from routine exchanges into opportunities for genuine connection, offering a shared experience that transcends time and leaves a lasting imprint on the participants involved.

Be present in your authenticity, understanding that it is not just a personal journey but a powerful catalyst for inspiring and enrolling others. Let the magic of authenticity unfold, and witness how it transforms relationships, kindles trust, and sparks the flame of involvement in the hearts of those who share in your vision and purpose.

Ajay Rawat

Honest advertisement

An example of effective enrollment comes from the advertising world: Ernest Shackleton's newspaper ad titled "Men Wanted for Hazardous Journey." This ad is highly regarded among copywriters and advertisers for its authenticity and honesty. Shackleton accurately portrayed the harsh conditions and dangers of the Antarctic expedition, without sugarcoating the reality.

Unlike many advertisements that overpromise and exaggerate product features, Shackleton's ad was straightforward and transparent. It effectively communicated the risks and challenges in a concise yet compelling manner, fostering trust and credibility.

The ad also highlights the importance of understanding the target audience and appealing to their motivations. Shackleton sought candidates who were undeterred by difficulties and motivated by honor and recognition. By capturing this message effectively, the ad attracted individuals who were genuinely interested and committed to the opportunity.

Empty Your Bags. Unlock Your Potential.

Additionally, the ad has been widely quoted and referenced in various contexts, from leadership and management to marketing and copywriting. Its enduring popularity and relevance demonstrate the power of authentic and honest communication in building trust, engagement, and loyalty among audiences.

The Shackleton "Men Wanted" advertisement was first quoted in Carl Hopkins Elmore's book Quit You Like Men in 1944, this book was published five years before the 100 Greatest Advertisements came out and made Shackleton's ad famous. In his book, Elmore describes how Sir Ernest Shackleton printed a statement in the papers when he was about to set out on one of his expeditions, seeking men for a hazardous journey to the South Pole. The statement read, "Small wages, bitter cold, long months of complete darkness, constant danger. Safe return doubtful. Honor and recognition in case of success." Apparently, Shackleton shared that the response to his appeal was overwhelming and it seemed as though all the men of Great Britain were determined to accompany him. This powerful ad has since been quoted many times by copywriters and advertisers as an example of the value of authenticity and honesty in recruitment and enrollment.

This clearly shows power of authenticity for enrollment because it can inspire and motivate people to get involved in a program or opportunity. By communicating personal stories and experiences, being transparent and honest, communicating values and mission, creating a sense of community and belonging, and celebrating success and achievements, enrollment efforts can become more powerful and effective.

The Shackleton advertisement exemplify how authentic communication can be effective in attracting the right candidates. In the ad, Shackleton was upfront and transparent about the challenges and risks involved in the journey, including small wages, bitter cold, long months of complete darkness, and constant danger.

The Shackleton advertisement serves as a great illustration of effective and authentic communication. Shackleton was transparent about the challenges and risks of the journey, such as small wages, bitter cold, long months of complete darkness, and constant danger. But he also promised that success would bring honor and recognition. They were drawn to the excitement of success and discovery.

Shackleton was able to create a strong and supportive relationship with his team by inviting them with transparency and authenticity. This strong relationship allowed the team to remain determined while they were on their journey, and they eventually accomplished their goal of exploring the Antarctic.

Empty Your Bags. Unlock Your Potential.

Tips for build strong relationships

Here are few tips here for how do you build strong and supportive relationships that can help you achieve your ambitious goals with help of enrolment and powerful communication:

1. Focus on building relationships, not just networking: Networking can be a great way to meet new people and expand your circle of contacts. However, it is important to focus on building real relationships with others, rather than just adding people to your list of contacts. Take the time to get to know others, listen to their stories, and find ways to support and help each other.

2. Maintain an authentic presence: When developing relationships, it is important to present yourself authentically. It is essential to be open and honest so that others can trust and respect you. Being genuine can help build strong connections between you and your peers.

3. Share your vision and goals: When you collaborate with others, it is important to share your vision and goals. This will help others understand what you are trying to achieve and how they can support you.

4. Show appreciation: When someone helps you or supports you, make sure to express your gratitude. Saying "thank you" goes a long way in building strong and supportive relationships.

5. Seek out like-minded individuals: When pursuing

Ajay Rawat

How to empty bag of heart?

Let go of assumptions and judgments: Creating enrolment requires having an open mind and being willing to listen to others. This means letting go of any assumptions or judgments you may have and approaching others with curiosity and respect. When you assume things about others or judge them based on limited information, it can create barriers to communication and understanding. Instead, take the time to listen to others and ask questions to gain a deeper understanding of their perspectives. By doing so, you can build trust and create a space for meaningful dialogue and collaboration.

Get rid of self-centeredness: Enrolment requires putting the needs and desires of others first. This means shifting your focus from yourself to others and finding out what motivates and inspires them. When you are self-centered, it can be difficult to connect with others and build relationships. Instead, focus on being empathetic and compassionate towards others. Take the time to listen to their needs and desires and find ways to support and encourage them. By doing so, you can build strong relationships and create a sense of community that inspires others to take action.

Empty out fear: Fear can hold you back from taking risks and pursuing your goals. When it comes to creating enrolment, fear can be a major obstacle. Try to identify any fears that may be preventing you from creating enrolment and find ways to overcome them. This could involve developing a mindset of growth and resilience, seeking support from others, or taking small steps towards your goal. When you let go of fear, you can tap into your creativity and passion, and inspire others to join you in pursuing a shared vision.

Drop resistance to change: Change is a natural part of life and can often lead to growth and new opportunities. However, it can also be scary and uncomfortable. When it comes to creating enrolment, it's important to let go of any resistance to change and be willing to embrace new ideas and perspectives. This could involve stepping outside of your comfort zone, being open to feedback and constructive criticism, and being willing to adapt and evolve as circumstances change. When you embrace change, you can inspire others to do the same, and create a culture of innovation and creativity.

Lose attachment to outcome: Creating enrolment is about inspiring others to take action, but you can't control their decisions. It's important to let go of any attachment to the outcome and focus on doing your best to create a positive impact. When you become attached to a specific outcome, it can lead to disappointment and frustration if things don't go as planned. Instead, focus on the process and the relationships you are building along the way. Celebrate small wins and learn from any setbacks. By doing so, you can create a sense of momentum and energy that inspires others to join you on the journey.

My suggestion is that instead of being attached to a specific outcome, focus on identifying what you believe to be the best way to achieve success. Celebrate and encourage individuals who are willing to contribute to the common goal that is important to you.

It's crucial to recognize that success isn't solely about achieving the desired outcome. It's also about the process of getting there and the relationships built along the way. Therefore, it's important to focus on building those relationships and encouraging others to join you on the journey.

By shifting your focus from attachment to the outcome to celebrating small wins and recognizing the contributions of others, you can create a sense of momentum and energy that inspires others to get involved. This can lead to a more significant impact on the common goal you are working towards.

Empty your HEART bag and adopt authenticity in communication and expression to enroll people in your goal or objective.

Exercise:
I invite you to take a moment to write down examples of Enrolments you must have done in your life. Given

Empty Your Bags. Unlock Your Potential.

below are two columns: one in which you list 10 instances where you enrolled people with verbal communication and caused results, and another in which you list instances of using non-verbal communication to enroll others in your purpose unknowingly.

We have to keep in mind this should not have instances where you had to manipulate things or fake things up

Enrolment with verbal communication	Enrolment with non-verbal communication

Ajay Rawat

Empty Your Bag Of Habits

Structures

Empty Your Bags. Unlock Your Potential.

The Psychology of Behaviour
How Our Thoughts and Actions Define Us

Have you ever found yourself stuck in the same situation again and again, wondering why you can't seem to break free from a pattern of doubt and uncertainty? I know I have. As a first-time trekker, I found myself repeating the same mistakes over and over again, getting tiered and finding it tough to move ahead often and lagging behind the group all the time, I was missing on lot of opportunities to explore new trails and pushing my limits, plus was not able to bond with fellow trekkers which is also very important.

It wasn't until I discovered the power of a support structure that I was able to move to the next phase of my trekking journey. With the help of a knowledgeable guide and a supportive group of fellow trekkers, I was able to identify and break free from the habits and behaviors that were holding me back. Together, we worked to overcome obstacles, push past our limits, and achieve our goals.

This experience taught me the importance of understanding our own habits and behaviors, and how they can impact our ability to build effective support structures. It's not just about breaking free from negative patterns - it's also about creating positive ones that help us to thrive and grow.

In this section of the book, we'll explore the science of habit formation and how it influences our actions and decisions. We'll examine the common patterns that can keep us stuck in a cycle of doubt and uncertainty, and provide practical strategies for breaking free and creating positive change. Whether you're a trekker like me or simply looking to improve your personal and professional life, this section will provide you with the tools you need to build a strong support structure and achieve your goals.

"Your beliefs shape your thoughts, which then color the words you speak. Your words, in turn, motivate the actions you take, which eventually become the habits you form. These habits then determine the values you hold, and the values you uphold ultimately determine the results you achieve in life - your destiny."

In this version of the statement, the concept of destiny is linked to the results you achieve in life. It suggests that your thoughts and beliefs play a vital role in shaping your actions and, in turn, the habits you form. Over time, these habits become your behavior, which ultimately determine the results you achieve in life.

By understanding the power of your beliefs and the impact they have on your actions and habits, you can take control of your life's outcomes and shape your destiny. This statement implies that if you want to change the course of your life, you must begin by examining your beliefs and thoughts and working to develop positive habits and values.

Empty Your Bags. Unlock Your Potential.

The statement suggests that your destiny is not predetermined but rather a product of your thoughts, beliefs, and actions. Your thoughts and beliefs shape the habits you form, which, in turn, shape your values. It is your values that ultimately determine the results you achieve in life - your destiny.

This statement can serve as a powerful reminder that you have control over your life's outcomes. By focusing on positive thoughts and beliefs, developing positive habits and values, and taking consistent, purposeful action, you can shape your destiny and achieve the results you desire.

Behaviour is an essential aspect of our lives that plays a crucial role in shaping our existence. We have seen how it is driven by our thoughts, beliefs, and values, which are all connected in a complex and interwoven system. In order to live a fulfilling and intentional life, it is important to understand this relationship and how it impacts our behaviour.

Ajay Rawat

Head, heart, and hands

People often refuge to motivation to correct or improve their behavior. Motivation is a crucial factor in influencing our behavior and driving us to take action towards our goals. People often rely on motivation to improve their behavior or make positive changes in their lives. Whether it's the desire to succeed, the need for acceptance, or the drive to achieve financial stability, our motivations can have a profound impact on the decisions we make and the actions we take.

We have learned about motivation and its two main forms in the previous chapter of this book: intrinsic and extrinsic. Intrinsic motivators are internal and come from within, such as a passion for a particular activity or a desire to learn and grow. Extrinsic motivators, on the other hand, come from external sources, such as rewards, recognition, or financial incentives.

Extrinsic motivators, while not as long-lasting as intrinsic motivators, can still have a significant impact on behavior. Financial incentives, for example, can motivate people to work harder or perform better in their jobs. However, it's important to recognize that extrinsic motivators can sometimes have negative effects, such as creating a culture of competition and reducing intrinsic motivation.

Empty Your Bags. Unlock Your Potential.

Intrinsic motivators are an essential part of human nature, and they can play a significant role in promoting behavior change and personal satisfaction. When we engage in activities that align with our values and interests, we are more likely to be motivated and sustained in our efforts. Intrinsic motivation can be defined as the drive to engage in an activity because it is inherently interesting and enjoyable, and it is associated with a sense of competence, autonomy, and relatedness.

When we talk about intrinsic motivation, we cannot overlook the importance of preparing the ground for it to take root. The first step is to fine-tune our belief system and how we perceive things. For example, if someone has a limiting belief about their ability to write, it will be difficult for them to cultivate intrinsic motivation for writing. Once a person changes their belief system, it can create a massive shift in how they think about a particular object, person, or situation. They will be able to see things in a new light and approach them with renewed enthusiasm.

Once the ground of our thoughts becomes fertile, the seed of new ideas can germinate. Intrinsic motivation can be cultivated through our thoughts and self-talk, and how we communicate our ideas to others and ourselves. When we communicate positively about our ideas, we are creating an environment that fosters intrinsic motivation. This can lead to a sense of accomplishment and personal satisfaction, which can be more fulfilling than any external reward or recognition.

With the right mindset and motivation in place, we can then take fruitful actions that lead to results. This can involve setting goals and taking steps towards achieving them, or simply engaging in activities that bring us joy and fulfillment. When we are intrinsically motivated, we are more likely to approach these actions with enthusiasm and dedication, which in turn can lead to greater success and fulfillment in life.

Intrinsic motivation can also lead to a sense of purpose and fulfillment in life. When we are engaged in activities that align with our values and passions, we feel a greater sense of meaning and satisfaction. This can contribute to overall well-being and happiness, as we feel a sense of purpose and fulfillment in our lives.

In simplified words we can say one need to align one's head, heart, and hands for greater success. The idea of aligning one's head, heart, and hands has been a recognized concept for thousands of years and is essential for achieving greater success. The ancient Indian epic, the Valmiki Ramayana, illustrates this concept through a conversation between Laxmana and Hanuman. Laxmana emphasizes the importance of mastering the head, heart, and hands, and Hanuman acknowledges that achieving harmony between these three elements can lead to unstoppable success.

Aligning one's head refers to having a clear and focused mind. It involves having a vision and direction for one's life and staying focused on that path. It means being able to think critically and creatively, making sound decisions based on reason and logic.

Aligning one's heart involves being in touch with one's emotions and desires. It means understanding what truly matters to oneself, what motivates and inspires oneself. It is about aligning one's actions with one's values and beliefs, as well as being compassionate and empathetic towards others.

So why not harness this ancient wisdom for your own growth and success? By aligning your thoughts, emotions, and actions, you can unlock your full potential and tackle any challenge that comes your way.

The head, heart, and hand analogy provides a useful framework for understanding this relationship. The head represents the cognitive aspect of our behaviour, driven by logic and reason. It receives and processes information, and is responsible for our thoughts and beliefs. The heart represents the emotional aspect of our behaviour, driven by feelings and desires. It is responsible for our passions and motivations, and shapes our values and desires. The hand represents the physical aspect of our behaviour, driven by action and results. It is responsible for our actions and habits, which shape our outcomes and experiences.

The relationship between these three aspects of behaviour is cyclical and interdependent. Our thoughts and beliefs shape our language, which is our choice of words, which in turn shapes our actions and habits. Our actions and habits further shape our thoughts and beliefs, creating a continuous feedback loop. This relationship is powerful and has a significant impact on our lives, and it is important to be mindful of how our thoughts and beliefs shape our behaviour.

One way to do this is by choosing our words carefully. We have learned about the power of words and how they shape our destiny. Our words have a profound impact on our thoughts and actions, and can greatly shape our experiences and outcomes. By choosing our words carefully, we can create a more positive and intentional mindset that aligns our thoughts, beliefs, and behaviors for greater success.

Negative and self-defeating language, such as "I can't do it" or "I'm not good enough," can reinforce negative beliefs about ourselves and lead to negative outcomes. On the other hand, positive and empowering language, such as "I can do it" or "I am capable and deserving of success," can reinforce positive beliefs and lead to more positive outcomes.

Becoming aware of the words we use and how they shape our thoughts and actions is an important step in cultivating a positive mindset. By reframing our language, we can better understand our own behavior and make more deliberate and intentional choices. For example, instead of saying "I don't have time" or "I'm too busy," we can reframe our language to say "I choose to prioritize other things" or "I am making time for this later." This shift in language can help us to better understand our own priorities and make intentional choices that align with our goals.

Empty Your Bags. Unlock Your Potential.

Our mindset, which is the lens through which we perceive and respond to the world around us, has a significant impact on our behavior. Our thoughts, beliefs, and values shape our mindset and influence how we interpret and react to situations. If our mindset is negative and self-limiting, it can hold us back from reaching our full potential and achieving our goals. On the other hand, a positive and growth-oriented mindset can empower us to take action towards our desired outcomes and overcome obstacles.

One way to cultivate a more positive and intentional mindset is by becoming more aware of our thoughts and beliefs. By noticing when we are engaging in negative self-talk or limiting beliefs, we can challenge them and replace them with more positive and empowering thoughts. For example, if we find ourselves thinking "I'm not good enough" or "I'll never be able to do that," we can challenge these thoughts by asking ourselves if they are really true and replacing them with more positive statements such as "I am capable of learning and growing" or "I can do anything I set my mind to."

Anyone can switch to a growth mindset, regardless of their background or current mindset. By focusing on the possibilities of growth and expansion, we can break free from limiting beliefs and behaviors and begin to see new opportunities and possibilities in our lives. It takes practice and dedication, but with time and effort, we can rewire our thinking and become more intentional in our actions and decisions.

Ajay Rawat

Joining hands
Building a strong support system

I mentioned that for my trek, I opted to join a group led by experienced individuals who had climbed the seven summits and possessed a military background. Additionally, we had the assistance of local guides and residents. Although this was our intended plan, the significance of having people by your side during the ascent of a mountain cannot be overstated. They assist in maintaining a steady pace, keeping track of rest and meal periods, hydrating, and conversing during the five-day climb. Engaging in conversation is particularly important as it helps to keep one's mind occupied and distracted from minor problems such as fatigue or soreness.

Thanks to this support structure, I was able to achieve something that I never thought was possible.

The book of Ecclesiastes in the Old Testament famously states, "Two are better than one, because they have a good return for their labor: If either of them falls down, one can help the other up. But pity anyone who falls and has no one to help them up" (Ecclesiastes 4:9-10).

The book of Ecclesiastes is part of the Old Testament, which is the first section of the Christian Bible. It is attributed to the authorship of King Solomon, who was renowned for his wisdom and is said to have written many of the Old Testament books.

The passage in Ecclesiastes 4:9-10 emphasizes the importance of companionship and mutual support in achieving success. It suggests that when people work together, they can accomplish more than they would alone, and that they can provide each other with help and encouragement when needed. The passage uses the analogy of two people working together, with one able to help the other up if they fall down. This can be interpreted as not only providing physical assistance but also emotional and mental support.

The passage also highlights the negative consequences of not having anyone to rely on. The phrase "pity anyone who falls and has no one to help them up" suggests that a lack of support can lead to despair and hopelessness. This idea is reinforced in the next verse, which states, "Also, if two lie down together, they will keep warm. But how can one keep warm alone?" (Ecclesiastes 4:11). This metaphorical image of warmth and comfort reinforces the importance of companionship and support in all aspects of life.

Ecclesiastes 4:9-10 is a powerful reminder of the value of working together and supporting one another. It is a timeless message that has resonated with people throughout history and across cultures, and continues to be relevant today in a wide range of contexts, from personal relationships to business and beyond.

As humans, we have the ability to develop our own capabilities and not rely on external resources to find happiness. Accumulating material possessions might give us a momentary sense of pleasure, but it does not necessarily lead to lasting happiness. Love and contentment are two examples of emotions that can be generated from within.

However, having dreams and aspirations that go beyond our individual capacities requires us to leverage the resources and time of others. Inspiring to involve people into our vision and goals can be a powerful tool to achieve success. It is important to remember that discipline is key to achieving our goals and keeping up the momentum is crucial. There may be times when obstacles, minor failures or hindrances may lead to giving up, but having a support structure can help us overcome such challenges.

As the saying goes, "two is better than one", and group momentum can be an effective way to keep discipline in place. The support and encouragement of like-minded individuals can make a significant difference in achieving our goals. Hence, it is essential to build a strong support network that can provide guidance and motivation when needed. In summary, by developing our own capabilities and leveraging the support of others, we can achieve great success in our personal and professional lives.

Building a Circle for Success

It's important to understand that success in life is not just about individual effort and hard work only. While these are crucial factors, they are only a part of the equation. Building a strong support system, through partnerships and relationships, is equally important to achieve your personal and professional goals.

In fact, there is popular saying" you are the sum of the five people you spend the most time with "

Some say it sum of seven people, anyways… The number five or seven in the statement "you are the sum of the five/seven people you spend the most time with" is not a scientifically proven fact, and the number is used more as a cultural reference. The idea behind the statement is that the people you surround yourself with can have a significant impact on your life, regardless of whether it is five, seven, or any other number.

The idea is that the attitudes, beliefs, and habits of the people you spend the most time with will influence your own thoughts, behaviors, and choices. It's important to be mindful of the people you spend time with and to actively seek out relationships with individuals who have positive qualities and values that align with your own.

One of the key benefits of having a strong support system is the simplification of life. By surrounding yourself with individuals who share your values and goals, you can reduce the amount of mental and emotional energy you expend on managing relationships. This allows you to focus your energy on what's truly important.

The journey of life is much easier when you have a supportive network to turn to. Having people in your life who understand you, believe in you and have your best interests at heart can make all the difference. It's important to remember that relationships should be built on mutual trust and respect, and that everyone involved should contribute in their own way.

In terms of Maslow's Hierarchy of Needs, partnerships can play a crucial role in helping us meet our emotional and social needs. Having a support system can also help us feel secure and valued, which in turn can lead to a more fulfilled life.

Our thoughts and actions have a significant impact on the relationships we build. By being mindful of our behaviour, we can ensure that we build positive relationships that will support us in our personal and professional lives. It's important to be open and honest with others, and to make an effort to understand their perspectives.

The art of enrolment is a critical aspect of building relationships. When we enroll others in our vision and goals, they are more likely to support us. This requires us to be clear about what we want and to effectively communicate our vision to others. It's also important to be willing to listen to their perspectives and to work together to achieve mutual goals.

Empty Your Bags. Unlock Your Potential.

Leveraging your strengths is also crucial in building partnerships. By recognizing and utilizing our skills and abilities, we can build relationships that are based on mutual respect and a shared understanding of what we can each bring to the table. This allows us to work together in a more effective and efficient manner.

Ultimately, the power of partnership lies in the ability to achieve more together than we could alone. By building a strong support system, we can tap into the collective strengths and resources of those around us to achieve our goals and live a more fulfilling life. It's important to remember that partnerships are not just about receiving support, but also about giving it. By being a supportive partner, we can help others achieve their goals, which in turn strengthens the relationships we have built.

Partnerships in various fields have proven to be incredibly powerful and successful. Whether it's in the arts, sports, or business, having the right partner can often lead to greater results than working alone. In this section, we'll take a closer look at some examples of successful partnerships and explore why they work so well.

In the world of theatre, partnerships between actors and directors are crucial to the success of a play. A great example of this is the collaboration between the legendary actor **Laurence Olivier** and director **Peter Hall**. Together, they created some of the most memorable productions in the history of British theatre. Olivier's powerful performances were elevated by Hall's insightful direction, and the partnership between the two remains one of the most celebrated in the history of theatre.

Even between two, having a good partner can make all the difference. Often, senior or more experienced actors will help guide their co-stars, giving cues and helping to elevate the overall performance of a play or movie. This can be especially important for younger actors who are still learning the ropes. A good partnership on set can make all the difference in creating a powerful and memorable performance.

Talking about motion pictures, we see so many great partners who make a super support structure for each other along with the teams.

Tom Hanks and **Steven Spielberg's** partnership is a prime example of a supportive structure in the film industry. Over the years, the two have collaborated on a number of critically acclaimed and commercially successful films, including "Saving Private Ryan", "Catch Me If You Can", and "The Terminal". Their partnership has produced some of the most memorable and impactful films of the past several decades.

One of the defining factors of their partnership is the mutual respect and support they have for each other's work. Tom Hanks is widely regarded as one of the greatest actors of his generation, known for his powerful and versatile performances. Meanwhile, Steven Spielberg is one of the most visionary directors of our time, with a unique talent for telling stories that resonate with audiences around the world. By bringing their individual strengths together, they have been able to create something truly remarkable.

In addition to their mutual respect, Tom Hanks and Steven Spielberg have a strong working relationship. Both are highly professional and have a deep understanding of the filmmaking process. This has allowed them to work together smoothly and effectively, bringing their collective vision to life on the big screen. The two are also known for their commitment to their work and their ability to bring the best out of each other.

Tom Hanks and Steven Spielberg's team is a shining example of a supportive structure in the film industry. Their mutual respect, strong working relationship, and complementary strengths have allowed them to create some of the most memorable and successful films of recent times. Their partnership is a testament to the power of collaboration and the importance of supporting each other in achieving shared goals. By working together, Tom Hanks and Steven Spielberg have been able to achieve more than they could have on their own and have left an indelible mark on the film industry.

The partnership between **Martin Scorsese** and **Robert De Niro** is considered one of the most iconic and successful in the film industry. Over the years, the two have collaborated on several critically acclaimed and commercially successful films, including "Mean Streets", "Taxi Driver", "Raging Bull", "Goodfellas",

"Cape Fear", "Casino", and "The Irishman". Their partnership has produced some of the most memorable performances and films of all time, and has helped to establish both Martin Scorsese and Robert De Niro as two of the most important figures in the industry.

One of the key factors in the success of their partnership is their mutual respect and support for each other's work. Martin Scorsese is considered one of the greatest directors of all time, known for his unique style, attention to detail, and powerful storytelling. Meanwhile, Robert De Niro is widely regarded as one of the greatest actors of his generation, known for his powerful and nuanced

performances. By working together, they have been able to bring out the best in each other, creating films that are both memorable and impactful.

In addition to their mutual respect, Martin Scorsese and Robert De Niro have a strong working relationship. They have a deep understanding of each other's creative vision and are able to work together seamlessly to bring their films to life. They are also known for their commitment to their work and their willingness to push each other to reach new heights. Through their partnership, Martin Scorsese and Robert De Niro have created a legacy that will endure for generations to come.

Martin Scorsese and Robert De Niro's team is one of the most celebrated and influential in the film industry. Their collaboration has produced some of the most iconic and critically acclaimed films in recent history. The two have worked together on numerous projects, each time elevating the other's performance and solidifying their place as two of the most important figures in the film industry. However, their partnership with Universal Pictures has been particularly successful, offering another layer of support structure to their collaboration. The result has been a string of box office hits that have consistently made more than double the business of their other collaborative work. From "Goodfellas" to "Cape Fear", "Casino", and "The Irishman", the Scorsese-De Niro duo's films with Universal Pictures have been widely acclaimed by audiences and critics alike. This partnership is a testament to the power of collaboration and the importance of supporting each other in achieving shared goals. Their legacy will continue to inspire future generations of filmmakers and actors.

From Indian film industry, **Amitabh Bachchan** and **Manmohan Desai** were one of the most successful actor-director duos in the Indian film industry. Their collaboration spanned over a decade and resulted in several blockbuster hits. Their partnership was characterized by their shared vision and understanding of what made a successful film, as well as their ability to bring out the best in each other.

Amitabh Bachchan was already a well-established actor in Bollywood when he started working with Manmohan Desai, but their collaboration helped to establish him as one of the biggest stars in the Indian film industry. The films they worked on together showcased Amitabh's versatility as an actor, and his ability to play a wide range of roles. On the other hand, Manmohan Desai was known for his ability to create engaging and entertaining films that appealed to audiences across India.

Their partnership was a defining moment in the history of Indian cinema. The films produced by this collaboration were not only commercial successes, but also captivated audiences with their engaging storylines, memorable music, and powerful performances by Amitabh. Their partnership produced some of the most iconic films in the history of Bollywood, including "Amar Akbar Anthony", "Mard", and "Parvarish". These films continue to be beloved by audiences to this day and are considered classics in the Indian film industry.

The success of this partnership helped to establish both Amitabh and Manmohan as major figures in the Indian film industry. Amitabh's powerful performances and Manmohan's visionary direction combined to create a unique and memorable experience for audiences. Their films were not just about entertainment, but also tackled important social issues and showcased Amitabh's versatility as an actor.

The Amitabh Bachchan - Manmohan Desai team remains one of the most celebrated and remembered in the history of Bollywood. Their films continue to captivate audiences with their engaging storylines, memorable music, and powerful performances by Amitabh, and their impact on the Indian film industry is still felt to this day.

Other such partnership was between **Dilip Kumar** and **Bimal Roy**. Dilip Kumar is widely considered one of the greatest actors in the history of Indian cinema, and his collaboration with Bimal Roy resulted in several critically acclaimed films. Their first film together, "Devdas", was released in 1955 and was followed by the hit film "Madhumati" in 1958. Bimal Roy's humanistic approach to filmmaking and Dilip Kumar's naturalistic acting style combined to create timeless films that are still popular with audiences today.

Another successful partnership is between **Shah Rukh Khan** and **Karan Johar**. Shah Rukh Khan is one of the biggest stars in the Indian film industry and his collaboration with Karan Johar has resulted in several commercially successful and critically acclaimed films. Their first film together, "Kuch Hota Hai", was released in 1998 and was followed by several other hit films such as "My Name is Khan" and "Dilwale". Their shared understanding of what makes a successful film and ability to bring out the best in each other has been key to their success.

Partnership between **David Dhawan** and **Govinda** is another example of a successful collaboration in the Indian film industry. David Dhawan is a prominent filmmaker and his partnership with actor Govinda resulted in several hit comedies. Their first film together, "Taaqatwar", was released in 1989 and was followed by other entertaining films such as "Aankhen" and "Hero No. 1". Their films were known for their humor, catchy music, and entertaining storylines and helped to establish Govinda as a leading actor in the industry.

In the world of music, the Beatles are considered one of the greatest and most influential bands of all time. The group consisted of four talented musicians, **John Lennon, Paul McCartney, George Harrison**, and **Ringo Starr**, who came together to create a unique sound that blended various musical styles. The Beatles' music captivated audiences around the world and helped to define a new era in popular music.

One of the key factors in the Beatles' success was the support structure within the band. Lennon and McCartney were two of the most talented songwriters of their time and their musical partnership was a major driving force behind the band's sound. However, they were supported by the musical skills of Harrison and Starr, who brought their own unique perspectives and talents to the mix. The result was a harmonious blend of musical styles and a sound that was unlike anything that had come before.

In addition to their musical skills, The Beatles also influenced popular culture in ways that went beyond their music. Their fashion sense and distinctive haircuts helped to create a new fashion trend that was embraced by young people all over the world. The Beatles' music and fashion styles reflected the changing times and helped to define the cultural zeitgeist of the 1960s.

Despite their individual success as solo artists, Lennon and McCartney never matched the global impact they had as part of The Beatles. As a group, The Beatles dominated the charts and cultural conversation for a decade, from the mid-1960s to the mid-1970s. Their music and fashion styles continue to inspire musicians and fans to this day, and their lasting impact on popular culture is a testament to the strength of the support structure within the band. The Beatles' ability to work together and bring out the best in each other is a true testament to their musical genius and the enduring legacy of their music.

Successful partnerships can also be found in the world of sports. Whether it's a doubles tennis match, a rowing team, or a basketball game, having the right partner can make all the difference in winning. Some of the most iconic partnerships in sports history include Magic Johnson and Kareem Abdul-Jabbar of the Los Angeles Lakers, Pele and Carlos Alberto of the Brazilian national soccer team, and Martina Navratilova and Pam Shriver in women's tennis. These partnerships have proven to be incredibly successful, with each player bringing their own unique skills to the table and working together to achieve great results.

The partnership between **Real Madrid** and **Cristiano Ronaldo** is a prime example of how a strong support system can lead to sustained success. When Ronaldo joined Real Madrid, he brought with him immense talent and skills. But it was the combination of his abilities with the support and resources of the club that allowed him to reach new heights and achieve incredible success.

During his nine years at Real Madrid, Ronaldo helped the team win four Champions League titles and two La Liga titles. This success was not only due to his individual achievements, but also to the efforts of the coaching staff, the management, and his fellow players who formed a solid partnership and created a winning culture. This support system allowed Ronaldo to perform at his best, and helped the team maintain a high level of performance year after year. The world is always changing, and things might be different when you read this book, like Ronaldo's playing style or his team or club partnerships. But let's hope that any changes that happen will be positive and good.

Formula One is another sport that requires a high level of collaboration between teams and drivers, and the success of a team is dependent on the performance of both. However, some teams and drivers have managed to achieve sustained success over the years.

One of the best examples of a successful F1 team is **Scuderia Ferrari**, which has won a record 16 Constructors' Championships and 15 Drivers' Championships. Throughout the years, Ferrari has had many successful drivers, including **Michael**

Empty Your Bags. Unlock Your Potential.

Schumacher, who won five consecutive Drivers' Championships with the team from 2000 to 2004.

Michael Schumacher found a strong support structure at Ferrari, which allowed him to showcase his talent and achieve sustained success over the years. With the support of the team, he was able to win five consecutive Drivers' Championships and establish himself as one of the greatest drivers in the history of the sport.

Michael Schumacher was also awarded the title of "Sportsman of the Decade" by the International Sports Press Association (AIPS) in the 2000s. This award recognized his outstanding achievements in the sport of Formula One during that decade, including seven World Championships and numerous records set.

Another successful team is **McLaren**, which has won 8 Constructors' Championships and 12 Drivers' Championships. McLaren has had many successful drivers over the years, including **Ayrton Senna**, who won three Drivers' Championships with the team, and **Lewis Hamilton**, who won his first two Championships with McLaren in 2008 and 2014.

Red Bull's Stratos jump from space was a landmark event in the history of human space exploration and extreme sports. The mission involved Austrian skydiver **Felix Baumgartner** jumping from a stratospheric balloon from an altitude of 39 km above the Earth's surface. The success of this mission was due to the collaboration of a number of support structures and wonderful teams.

It was a testament to the power of collaboration and the importance of having strong support structures in place when attempting something truly extraordinary.

The statement "What all the big countries could not do by their space scientists was made possible by a private company" is misleading, as the Stratos jump was not a conventional space mission. However, it acknowledges the strong support team assembled by Red Bull that gave Felix Baumgartner the confidence and trust to attempt the jump. The collaboration of various teams, including the Engineering Team, Balloon Team, Mission Control Team, Medical Team, and Communications Team, was essential in making the Red Bull Stratos jump a success. The successful collaboration is a testament to the power of teamwork and the importance of having a solid support system when attempting something extraordinary.

Partnerships in business have proven to be incredibly powerful and successful. Some of the most successful business partnerships in history include **Steve Jobs** and **Steve Wozniak of Apple**, Bill Gates and Paul Allen of Microsoft, and Ben Cohen and Jerry Greenfield of Ben & Jerry's ice cream. In each of these partnerships, the two partners brought different skills and strengths to the table, working together to create something greater than what either could have accomplished alone. This is the power of partnership in a nutshell - by combining forces, partners can achieve much more than they could alone.

Empty Your Bags. Unlock Your Potential.

Steve Jobs and Steve Wozniak were two friends who had a passion for technology. J

Their partnership proved to be a winning combination, with Jobs' creativity and marketing skills, and Wozniak's technical expertise. Together, they created a company that revolutionized the personal computer industry and changed the way we live and work. The Apple I was followed by the Apple II, which was one of the first successful personal computers and helped establish Apple as a major player in the technology world. The partnership between Jobs and Wozniak was one of the key factors in the success of Apple and helped lay the foundation for the company's future success.

Throughout the years, the company continued to innovate and create new products, including the Macintosh, the iPod, the iPhone, and the iPad. With each new product, the company pushed the boundaries of what was possible and created a new standard in the technology world. This would not have been possible without the partnership and friendship between Jobs and Wozniak.

Their partnership was not just limited to the creation of new products, but also to the company's culture and values. Jobs and Wozniak had a shared vision for the company and worked together to create a company culture that was centered around creativity, innovation, and excellence. This culture has been a key factor in the company's continued success and has helped to attract top talent to the company.

Similarly, **Bill Gates** and **Paul Allen** co-founded Microsoft and went on to revolutionize the computer software industry. Their partnership was built on mutual respect and trust, and they were able to complement each other's strengths. Gates provided the business acumen and vision, while Allen brought his technical expertise to the table. They also had a shared commitment to innovation and excellence, which allowed them to develop and release industry-defining products such as MS-DOS and Windows.

This partnership was not only about work, but also about friendship. The two men had a close bond, and their shared experiences and challenges helped to forge a strong partnership that lasted for decades. Their partnership was not without its challenges, but they were able to overcome these obstacles and continue to drive the company forward.

Today, Microsoft remains one of the most valuable companies in the world, and the partnership between Gates and Allen is remembered as one of the most successful and influential in the history of technology. This is a testament to the power of partnership and the impact that it can have on both individuals and organizations.

In the field of science, partnerships are also a critical component of progress. One example is the partnership between **Watson** and **Crick**, who together discovered the structure of DNA. Their partnership was critical to the success of their discovery, as they were able to bring together their complementary skills and expertise to make a ground-breaking discovery that has since had a profound impact on the world of science.

I had an opportunity to travel to France and Italy as my creative pilgrimage. These two countries were the cradles of the Renaissance. There I witnessed the impactful partnerships shaping the world of art.

Art is often perceived as an individual affair, but one can truly see how art thrives on partnership. Partnerships between the Church, chapels, banks, and artists played pivotal roles during the Renaissance.

The Church and chapels were patrons of renowned Renaissance artists like **Leonardo da Vinci** and **Michelangelo**. Works such as Leonardo's Last Supper and Michelangelo's Sistine Chapel ceiling, celebrated masterpieces, conveyed religious messages, and showcased the Church's wealth and power. This partnership enabled artists to focus on their craft, receiving financial support and prestige in return.

Beyond financial backing, the Church supported artists through training and apprenticeships. Young talents learned from experienced masters, honing their skills to become successful artists in their own right.

During my travel, I explored the Louvre Museum in Paris, marveling at the Mona Lisa, and ventured to the Vatican City, where Michelangelo's Sistine Chapel work evoked profound awe. These two great artists are iconic names synonyms to the Renaissance.

However, if you step back in the timeline, you will find other masters paving the way to establish the Renaissance. One of them is **Sandro Botticelli**. Botticelli revolutionized the art scene in the 1400s, the early Renaissance period. It was fascinating to know how a not-so-known name fueled this whole art movement, the affluent Medici family in Florence, Italy. Starting from **Lorenzo de' Medici**, the Medici family supported many artists like Sandro Botticelli, marking the genesis of the Renaissance.

Florence city is a living canvas of Renaissance architecture and art. One of the must-visit places for art lovers is the Uffizi Museum. Here, the works of great masters, including Botticelli, *Caravaggio,* Raphael, and many more luminaries are exhibited. This partnership between banks, churches, and artists, as witnessed in Florence, catalyzed an art movement that influenced societal thinking and functioning, leaving an enduring impact.

The Medici family's support became a testament to the symbiosis of art and patronage. Without such structures, iconic masterpieces like the Mona Lisa, the

Empty Your Bags. Unlock Your Potential.

Last Supper, the Fall of Man, and the Birth of Venus might never have graced the world.

As I traversed these cultural landscapes, the resonance of collaborative efforts echoed through the centuries. The power of partnerships during the Renaissance, far from being a relic of the past, continues to inspire art, music, and writing globally. This enduring legacy reinforces the notion that, even in the realm of individual creativity, the strength of partnership and patronage remains an integral force, fostering the creation of timeless masterpieces.

Ajay Rawat

How our brain works for partnership

Yes, there is a brain science aspect to the formation of support structures. Research in neuroscience has shown that social interaction and connection are deeply ingrained in the human brain and that the brain is hardwired for social interaction and support.

For example, studies have shown that the release of oxytocin, a hormone associated with bonding and social interaction, increases when individuals engage in positive social interactions and form social connections. This suggests that the formation of support structures is not only driven by psychological and emotional needs, but also by biological factors.

Additionally, research has shown that the brain processes social information differently than other types of information, and that the brain is equipped with specific regions and neural networks that are dedicated to processing social information. This indicates that the brain is specifically designed to support social interaction and connection.

Furthermore, research has also shown that social support can have a positive impact on the brain and overall well-being. For example, studies have shown that social support can reduce stress and improve mood, and that it can also enhance cognitive function, such as memory and attention.

From my personal experience, I can attest to the power of a supportive structure, whether it be from family, workplace, creative endeavors, or in my case, my fitness journey. Before joining an online fitness community, I was struggling with my physical appearance and overall health due to weight gain during the pandemic and lockdown. However, with the help of the supportive community, I was able to make a significant transformation.

The community was filled with individuals who had similar goals and stories, and I was able to connect with them and share my own experiences. The support I received from the group was unparalleled, and I was never alone on my journey. The fitness professionals in the community provided me with expert guidance on my workout routines and nutrition, allowing me to learn and grow in a way that I never could have on my own.

The community also held me accountable and kept me motivated. I was able to share my progress and receive encouragement from my peers, which helped me to stay on track. The sense of community and friendship I gained from the group was invaluable, making the experience much more enjoyable.

Thanks to the support structure provided by the fitness community, I was able to shed 15 kgs in just three months and maintain my weight loss for 6 months and counting. I am now a healthier, happier, and more confident person. I firmly believe that with the right support, anyone can achieve their fitness goals and live a healthy and fulfilling life, and my personal experience is proof of that.

Building a strong support system through partnerships is critical for personal and professional success. By leveraging our strengths and working together with others, we can simplify our lives, meet our needs, and achieve more than we could alone. So, make an effort to build and nurture your partnerships, and watch as your life transforms for the better.

Modelling and mirroring

Modelling and mirroring is a strategy that involves emulating the behavior, mindset, and actions of successful individuals who have already accomplished what we aspire to achieve. By observing and learning from their experiences, we gain a reference point and a proven path to success, allowing us to avoid getting lost in a sea of options and uncertainty. Many coaches and trainers in the field of personal development, often emphasizes the importance of modelling in his teachings. They highlight that by learning from those who have already achieved success, we can accelerate our own progress and increase our chances of reaching our goals.

Tony Robbins, world famous coach and motivational speaker has extensively discussed the concept of modelling and its impact on personal growth and success. He emphasizes that successful individuals have specific strategies, beliefs, and behaviors that contribute to their achievements. By studying and adopting these qualities, we can shape our own path towards success. Robbins advises aspiring individuals to identify a role model who embodies the success they desire and learn from their experiences. He suggests studying their mindset, behavior patterns, and strategies, and incorporating these into our own lives.

Robbins also highlights the importance of actively seeking mentorship from successful individuals. By surrounding ourselves with individuals who have achieved what we aspire to, we expose ourselves to their wisdom, guidance, and positive influence. This process of modelling and mirroring helps to expand our possibilities and tap into our full potential.

Books, podcasts, and videos are some other means to connect indirectly with those successful individuals, where they allow us peek in their thinking minds.

The concept of modelling and mirroring can be traced back to ancient philosophers and thinkers. Aristotle, an influential philosopher of those time, emphasized the importance of emulating virtuous individuals to cultivate one's own character and behavior. He believed that by observing and modelling ourselves after morally upright individuals, we can refine our own virtues and improve our chances of success.

All these ideas and concepts are rooted in Neuro-Linguistic Programming and Modelling

Neuro-Linguistic Programming (NLP) provides further insights into the effectiveness of modelling and mirroring. NLP explores how our thoughts, language, and behaviors shape our experiences. According to NLP, by mirroring the actions, language patterns, and physiology of successful individuals, we can tap into their mindset and replicate their strategies. This process helps reprogram our own neurology and enhances our ability to achieve success.

NLP techniques such as matching and mirroring involve adopting the non-verbal behaviors, vocal patterns, and language of our role models. By doing so, we establish rapport and connect with them on a deeper level. This connection allows us to absorb their wisdom and integrate it into our own lives more effectively.

Modelling and mirroring provides a valuable approach for individuals who lack a supportive circle or struggle to enroll others in their pursuit of success. The principles of Neuro-Linguistic Programming further support the effectiveness of modelling and mirroring by highlighting the impact of our thoughts, language, and behaviors on achieving success. By embracing this concept, we empower ourselves to shape our own journey and increase our chances of attaining the success we aspire to.

Ajay Rawat

Aspirational Behavior Blueprint

There is another school of thought which help us break away from our limiting patterns which compel us to take same old actions and expecting different results. No wonder we find ourselves trapped in similar circumstances which then further strengthens our believes about our inability to cause a different result. We can call this new methodology "Aspirational Behavior Blueprint". In this methodology we examine what really inspire and excite us, something that we want in our future. But the beauty is, we pull that distant future to now and behave in a way that is aligned to that future. In this keep checking if our action will result in that future or not. Anything that we see not contributing the future in now, we can avoid.

Some people refer to similar methodologies as fake it till you make it. A popular quote that lot of young achievers give credit to their success, knowing little about the neuro science behind this, which is in the domain on neuroplasticity.

Neuroplasticity refers to the brain's ability to adapt and reorganize itself in response to new experiences and learning. When we engage in "faking it" or adopting a new behavior, our brain's neural circuits are activated. With repetition and practice, these circuits become strengthened and more automatic, leading to a genuine transformation in our mindset and abilities.

Empty Your Bags. Unlock Your Potential.

Research in neuroscience has shown that our thoughts and emotions are intricately connected to our physiology. By intentionally adopting a mindset associated with confidence or competence, we can influence our brain chemistry and emotional state. This can lead to increased self-belief and reduced anxiety, enabling us to perform better in challenging situations.

Moreover, embodying a certain behavior, even if initially forced or insincere, can elicit positive responses from others. These external affirmations and social feedback can further reinforce our own perception and confidence, creating a positive feedback loop.

A similar concept is very beautifully presented in bestselling "Atomic Habits" by James Clear. The book that explores the power of small habits and incremental changes in achieving personal growth and success. The book emphasize the importance of designing systems and structures to shape one's behavior and identity.

Clear introduces the idea of identity-based habits, which involves adopting the mindset and behaviors of the person one wants to become. By aligning one's actions with the identity of the desired future self, individuals create a support structure that reinforces positive habits and propels them towards their goals.

The process of identity-based habits starts with clarifying the desired identity and envisioning the characteristics of that person. This includes understanding their values, beliefs, and habits. By intentionally integrating small, consistent habits into daily routines, individuals gradually build momentum towards embodying their desired identity.

Creating these structures and systems involves leveraging cues, cravings, and rewards to establish positive habits. Clear suggests making habit implementation obvious, attractive, easy, and satisfying. By making desired actions more visible, appealing, and effortless, individuals increase the likelihood of adopting these behaviors.

By implementing identity-based habits and designing supportive structures, individuals are not solely relying on willpower and motivation to drive their actions. They are building a sustainable foundation that aligns with their desired future self. These structures and systems provide ongoing support and reinforcement, making it easier to maintain positive habits and progress towards their goals.

Identity-based habits can be a significant support structures to cultivate positive behaviors and achieve success. This also help people to inculcate those value systems which made those people successful and that is why they became your role model. It is important as this help you grow from grounds up than being enamoured by the spectacle of their success without understanding the hard work, persistence and value system responsible for that success.

Empty Your Bags. Unlock Your Potential.

Exercise:
Take a moment to reflect on the support structures in your life. Think about the individuals who you turn to for help, encouragement, and guidance. These could be friends, family members, co-workers, or a supportive community. Show your gratitude to these important people by reaching out and expressing your thanks. Give them a call or send a message to let them know just how much they mean to you. Building strong support structures is crucial for our well-being and personal growth, and it's never too late to acknowledge and appreciate those who play a role in our lives. Join me in taking the time to show our gratitude to the people who support us.

Ajay Rawat

Empty Your Bag Of Know-Hows

Back to dreams

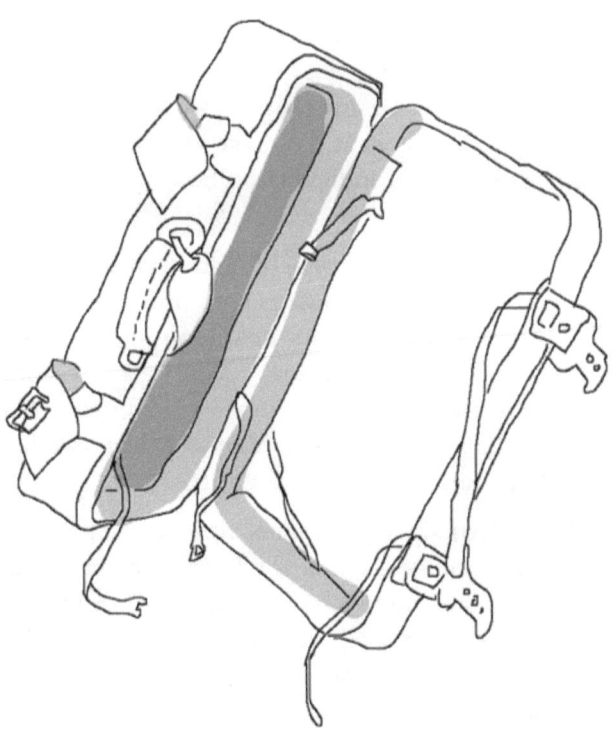

Are you thinking that you've
ARRIVED?

Settling for what you have achieved can be a tempting trap to fall into. You may feel content with your current situation and be hesitant to push yourself to strive for something more. However, the dangers of settling for what you have achieved cannot be ignored. In this chapter, we will discuss the risks of settling for what you have accomplished and provide examples of individuals who have fallen into this trap.

One of the biggest risks of settling for what you have achieved is stagnation. When you become content with your current situation, you may stop growing and developing as an individual. You may become complacent and lack the motivation to pursue new goals and challenges. This can ultimately lead to a lack of fulfillment and purpose in your life.

Another risk of settling for what you have achieved is missed opportunities. When you become content with your current situation, you may fail to recognize new opportunities that present themselves. You may be too comfortable to take risks and try something new, which can prevent you from achieving even greater success.

One example of an individual who fell into the trap of settling for what they had achieved is former NBA basketball player Michael Jordan. After winning three NBA championships in a row, Jordan shocked the world by announcing his retirement from basketball. He had accomplished what many considered to be the pinnacle of success in his field, and many believed he had nothing left to prove. However, after a brief stint playing professional baseball, Jordan returned to the NBA and led his team to three more championships. This is a prime example of how settling for what you have achieved can prevent you from reaching even greater heights of success.

A contrasting example of an individual who overcame the trap of settling is former United States President Barack Obama. After serving two terms as president, Obama could have easily retired from public service and lived a comfortable life. However, he recognized the importance of continuing to push himself and set new goals. He has since launched various initiatives aimed at promoting civic engagement and empowering young leaders. By refusing to settle for what he had achieved, Obama continues to make a positive impact on the world.

It is important to recognize that settling for what you have achieved is not just a risk for high achievers like Jordan and Obama. It is a risk for anyone who is content with their current situation and hesitant to push themselves to strive for something more. Whether it's in your personal or professional life, settling for what you have achieved can prevent you from experiencing new opportunities and growing as an individual.

To avoid this trap of settling for what you have achieved, it is important to continually challenge yourself and set new goals. This does not necessarily mean that you need to make drastic changes in your life. It can simply mean setting small goals and taking steps towards achieving them. This can help you to maintain a sense of purpose and motivation in your life.

In addition, it is important to maintain a growth mindset. This means embracing challenges and seeing failures as opportunities for growth and learning. When you approach life with a growth mindset, you are less likely to become complacent and more likely to seek out new opportunities for growth and development.

Continual growth and development are crucial for achieving success, both in our personal and professional lives. It requires effort, dedication, and a willingness to step out of our comfort zones. However, it's essential to be mindful that the new knowledge of 'now I know, how to get results' can become the new comfort zone, leading us to settle for what we have achieved. Therefore, we must remain watchful and strive to avoid complacency.

By setting new goals and seeking out new challenges, we can broaden our horizons and open up new possibilities. Each new experience provides an opportunity for growth and development, which can help us become better versions of ourselves. It's also crucial to surround ourselves with people who challenge and motivate us, helping us stay inspired and committed to our goals. We have learned about circle of success in one of the previous chapters.

Through continuous growth and development, we can improve our skills, knowledge, and abilities, which can benefit us in various aspects of our lives. We become more confident, resilient, adaptable, and better equipped to face new challenges. It also provides us with a sense of purpose and fulfillment, which can positively impact our mental and emotional well-being.

To avoid complacency, we must be willing to step out of our comfort zones and challenge ourselves to learn and grow continually. It can be helpful to set new goals regularly and identify areas where we can improve. Seeking feedback from others and taking on new challenges can also provide valuable opportunities for growth and development.

The human brain, just like the body, has a limited capacity for processing information. When we consume more knowledge than we can utilize, we experience a mental overload, which can hinder our ability to think clearly and make decisions. This excess knowledge becomes like excess food in the body that cannot be broken down and is stored as unnecessary fat.

To avoid accumulating unnecessary knowledge, it is essential to focus on practical application. Knowledge that is not applied is of little use and can lead to a sense of overwhelm and confusion. In contrast, knowledge that is applied through action can help solidify concepts, develop new skills, and achieve goals.

Ajay Rawat

Unleashing the Power to Dream Again: A Journey to True Freedom

In the intricate tapestry of our human endeavors, we've ventured into the labyrinth of dreams, discovering how these ethereal aspirations form the genesis of our pursuits. Yet, there exists a profound layer waiting to be unveiled—a layer that transcends the confines of conventional dreams, a layer that embodies the essence of true freedom. As we navigate this exploration, we unearth the transformative power that dreaming again holds, delving into the intricacies of a free mind and the boundless possibilities it envisions.

I've previously illuminated the potential trap that 'know-hows' can set, not only in our thinking, planning, and actions but, more crucially, in our capacity to dream. Our journey began by understanding dreams in their fundamental role in steering our human endeavors. Now, let's embark on a deeper exploration—a journey into the next level of freedom, the power to dream again.

Consider the dreams we've discussed so far—often entwined with goals and ambitions, shaped by external benchmarks and societal expectations. These dreams, while significant, are tethered to reference points and influenced by perceptions of success and achievement. In essence, they are relative, a reflection of what others have set as benchmarks. But there exists a realm of dreams untouched by restrictions or external influences—a realm that only a free mind can explore.

True dreams, I posit, are those that emerge without any constraints, untainted by fears or preconceived notions. These are the dreams that flow from a liberated mind, unshackled from the chains of societal norms and previous references. To dream again becomes a manifestation of the next level of freedom—an evolution beyond the so-called dreams that are, in reality, goals, and ambitions validated by external standards.

The power to dream again signifies a shift from proving oneself to others to seeking authenticity and pursuing aspirations untouched by external influences. It beckons individuals to step into the arena of their real dreams, unburdened by the weight of fear or the shadows of past references. This is where true power resides.

Imagine a scenario akin to a sportsperson with a specific target, record, or victory in mind. Once that milestone is achieved, a realization dawns—they are running toward something doable, something within the confines of a perceived reality. However, the journey doesn't end there. Instead, a new target emerges, and then another, creating a continuous cycle of discovery—a journey into the next level of power, the power to dream, the power to be free.

To dream again, therefore, becomes a process of self-discovery and continual liberation. It is an acknowledgment that what was once perceived as important or indispensable might no longer hold the same weight. It's a conscious shedding of layers, akin to a butterfly emerging from its cocoon, revealing new facets of potential and untapped possibilities.

In essence, the power to dream again unveils the supreme nature of a free human mind. It is the recognition that true freedom extends beyond physical constraints—it encompasses mental and spiritual liberation. Only when the body, mind, and soul are free can dreams manifest in their purest form. Otherwise, what might seem like a dream is, in reality, a thought, a goal, or something influenced by external perceptions.

The supreme aspect lies in the ability to dream with a liberated mind, detached from societal expectations or preconceived notions of success. It is about embracing the uncertainty of uncharted dreams, where the journey itself becomes the destination, and the process of discovery is as significant as the dreams realized.

To dream again, therefore, is to strip away the layers of conformity, societal conditioning, and past references. It is to embrace the vulnerability of the unknown and find strength in the uncharted territories of one's authentic desires. This continual process of dreaming anew serves as a constant reminder of the evolving nature of freedom—a freedom that transcends the known, unlocking the infinite potential within.

Turning dreams into reality is about having a clear vision and the courage to take action. Taking action is crucial for success. It's the key to overcoming procrastination.

When you have ambitious dreams, break them into smaller goals and tasks. Take small, consistent steps. These little actions give you a sense of accomplishment and push you forward. They build momentum and boost your confidence. Making your dreams come true feels less overwhelming when you're committed to making steady progress in a planned and measurable way. Remember those S. M. A. R. T. goals?

Learning(again) is another important part of taking action. By focusing on areas that directly connect to your goals, you make the knowledge you gain even more powerful. Understand the details of what you're trying to achieve and use your newfound wisdom effectively. This way you make your actions more impactful on the journey to turning your dreams into reality.

In simple terms, to make your dreams come true, you need a clear vision, courage to take action, and a commitment to steady progress. Break your big goals into smaller tasks, take consistent steps, and prioritize learning in areas that align with your goals. This way, your actions become a powerful force on the path to realizing your dreams.

Ajay Rawat

So, how much do you pack for your travel?

When I returned from the trek and began unpacking my bags, I realized that there were a couple of things that I never used during the entire trip, and then there were a few that were not even opened or unpacked, which I luckily could return to the stores.

But I kept wondering why I even packed them in the first place.

Had I not returned my unused items from the trek they would have been a waste for me and taking space in my house eating dust for months and year before they could be used again and you know if you try to use anything after a year or so 99% chances it won't work and you discard that to buy new stuff.

Why only trek and trek related stuff, there are so many other things in my house which are stored and not being used, consuming space and eating dust.

I recently got some repairs and whitewash done at my place and it is a herculean task to get stuff together, pack them, get the work done, unpack stuff and rearrange them again. And in that process, there are more than million times you keep questioning if I need this thing now or in future, to keep it or throw it. For me it was even tougher as I was staying in the house when the repairs and whitewash was going on. So, the ordeal was to keep shifting entire stuff from one room to another till the next room's turn comes. In that process the number of times you ask this question gets at least double if not triple. And you lose, and break things in the process…which further adds to the list of items to be thrown as waste. This was the case of one family, smallest unit of our society and multiply it with a few billions and you can imagine the magnitude of waste we accumulate and keep on accumulating for ourselves and our future generations. That has made those landfill mountains a common sight in our cities, you don't see clean rivers, and clear sky? Do you remember when did you last see a clear blue sky in your city or town?

Governments are struggling big time to manage this waste problem. Lot of corporates take it up as their Corporate Social Responsibility initiatives to support and contribute, and I am sure many individuals do take up such tasks and are willing to contribute to solve for the global issue but none of them individually or even collectively can fight this challenge, they can't match to speed it is growing causing so much of ecological imbalance and climate change which is impacting marine life and melting glaciers.

While cities and states do take measures but they do it within their limits and have limited reach, it is tough when you have to deal with this at a country level. Look at Maldives the whole country is on the verge of getting submerged due to climate change and sea level rising. And I am sure with very little fault of theirs, being a small country with islands they are not generating that much of waste or pollution but all countries collectively including Maldives are impacting the global challenge.

Like I said if there is something in a specific region or country, one can blame it to the respective country but what if the problem is due to a geographical phenomenon, with no specific country to be blamed for. This great pacific garbage patch is an example of this problem, when the ocean tides brings all the garbage in a specific region, which is floating there for god knows how long.

The Great Pacific Garbage Patch is a zone in the Pacific Ocean between Hawaii and California where plastic waste has accumulated. The size of the garbage patch is difficult to measure because the debris constantly moves. However, a major study in 2018 estimate the patch covers an estimated surface area of 1.6 million square kilometres, an area twice the size of Texas or three times the size of France. The Great Pacific Garbage Patch is the best known of several such zones. Others exist in the Atlantic and Indian oceans.

The debris in the Great Pacific Garbage Patch comes mainly from the west coasts of North and South America and the east coasts of China and other Asian countries. Wind and currents carry the garbage into the North Pacific subtropical gyre. A gyre is a large area with rotating ocean currents. The clockwise rotation of the gyre draws in and traps solid matter such as plastics.

Some 80 percent of the plastics in the garbage patch come from the land. It takes years for debris to travel from the coasts to the gyre. As the garbage is carried along, sunlight, wind, and waves cause some of the plastics to break down into tiny, nearly invisible bits. Therefore, the Great Pacific Garbage Patch is not a solid block of compacted plastic. Instead, it contains a mixture of larger objects and a soup of microplastics. The dimensions and depth of the patch are continuously changing.

Not only does plastic pollution in the Great Pacific Garbage Patch pose risks for the safety and health of marine animals, but there are health and economic implications for humans as well.

Fishing nets account for 46% of the mass in the GPGP and they can be dangerous for animals who swim or collide into them and cannot extract themselves from the net. Interaction with these discarded nets, also known as ghost nets , often results in the death of the marine life involved.

Through a process called bioaccumulation, chemicals in plastics will enter the body of the animal feeding on the plastic, and as the feeder becomes prey, the chemicals will pass to the predator – making their way up the food web that includes humans. These chemicals that affected the plastic feeders could then be present within the human as well.

According to a study conducted in collaboration with Deloitte, yearly economic costs due to marine plastic are estimated to be between $6-19bn USD. The costs stem from its impact on tourism, fisheries and aquaculture, and (governmental) clean-ups. These costs do not include the impact on human health and the marine ecosystem (due to insufficient research available). This means that intercepting plastic in rivers is much more cost-effective than dealing with the consequences downstream.

The ocean plastic problem has led to numerous efforts to clean up the Great Pacific Garbage Patch. Among these, Ocean Voyages Institute's Project Kaisei has been successful in removing significant amounts of plastic from the ocean during multiple expeditions, setting records in 2019 and 2020 for the largest clean up in the Garbage Patch. In 2022, the initiative removed 134 tons of plastic debris from the Garbage Patch. Meanwhile,

The Ocean Clean up Project has been deploying various systems to collect plastic from the gyre since 2018, with its System 002 collecting 63,182 pounds of plastic in 2021. The initiative recently announced the transition to System 03, which is claimed to be 10 times as effective as its predecessor.

"Turning our attention to land, we encounter another massive challenge - the cleanup of Mount Everest. Just as the Pacific Garbage Patch is a glaring example of ocean pollution, Everest's slopes bear the scars of decades of climbing expeditions. Piles of discarded gear, plastic waste, and human waste have accumulated, marring the pristine beauty of the world's highest peak.

Empty Your Bags. Unlock Your Potential.

Cleaning up Mount Everest is a mission that demands our commitment to preserving not only natural beauty but also the delicate Himalayan ecosystem. The effort involves removing tons of waste left behind by climbers over the years.

Why only land and sea, we humans have taken this to space as well. It is estimated that there are about 200,000 pieces between 1 and 10 cm (0.4 and 4 inches) across and that there could be millions of pieces smaller than 1 cm. How long a piece of space debris takes to fall back to Earth depends on its altitude.

Space debris, also known as space junk, refers to the objects floating in outer space that no longer have a function, such as spent rocket stages, defunct satellites, and broken bits from spacecraft and other space equipment. The issue of space debris has been increasing due to the rapid growth of space technology and the increasing number of space missions. According to the European Space Agency (ESA), there have been over 560 fragmentation incidents since 1961, with most of them caused by fuel explosions in rocket stages. Although there have only been seven direct collisions, it is the small fragments that pose the greatest danger.

Micrometeorites like paint flakes and solidified droplets of antifreeze can damage solar panels on active satellites, while other dangerous debris includes vestiges of solid fuel that float about in space and are highly flammable. Moreover, some Russian satellites contain nuclear batteries with radioactive material that could cause dangerous contamination if they returned to Earth. The rising population of space debris increases the potential danger to all space vehicles, including the International Space Station and other spacecraft with humans aboard, such as SpaceX's Crew Dragon.

NASA takes the threat of collisions with space debris seriously and has a long-standing set of guidelines on how to deal with each potential collision threat to the space station. These guidelines specify when the expected proximity of a piece of debris increases the probability of a collision enough that evasive action or other precautions to ensure the safety of the crew are needed.

To combat the issue of space debris, various solutions have been developed. One such strategy is to change the orbit of the satellites, launching them into elliptical orbits with perigees within the Earth's atmosphere, causing them to break up eventually. Another solution is self-destruction, which involves programming the satellite to leave its orbit at the end of its useful life and be eliminated when it comes into contact with the atmosphere. Passivation is another method used to remove any internal energy contained in the vehicle at the end of its useful life. Although the chassis remains in orbit, there is less risk of explosions.

SpaceX, the aerospace company owned by Elon Musk, has developed a reuse strategy where rockets return to Earth intact. This helps in reducing the amount of debris left in space. Lasers are also being considered to vaporise the surface of fragments, which causes them to fall and stop them.

Although the issue of space debris is concerning, the positive outlook is that humans have become responsible in cleaning up and managing space debris. In 2021, a demonstration mission by ClearSpace SA, a Swiss start-up, was launched to capture and remove a piece of debris from space. Moreover, in 2022, the United States Space Force demonstrated the use of a robotic arm to remove debris in space. These initiatives show that humans are taking the necessary steps to reduce space debris and ensure the safety of space vehicles and astronauts.

This could possibly be a balanced approach to keep the development and researches going on yet keeping the issue of waste generation under control.

A balanced approach is necessary, which involves limiting the production of additional debris while actively removing existing debris. Spacecraft and satellites must be equipped with protective measures, and end-of-life disposal strategies need to be implemented.

The painting of the Golden Gate Bridge is a practical example of mindful development. They regularly paint the bridge in a reddish orange, to ensure that it can be seen through the fog that forms over the bay. However, a crucial step in this process is the meticulous removal of the old layer of paint before applying a fresh coat.

Scraping the old paint off the Golden Gate Bridge is essential. The new paint on top of the existing layers would strain the bridge too much. This is due to the fact that the paint contains approximately 80% metal, effectively adding a thin layer of metal throughout the entire structure.

The bridge would get an additional weight of 250 tons with metal rich paint. Such a substantial increase in weight might cause serious issues and compromise the bridge's structure.

The bridge may not be able to handle such a large weight increase. To avoid these risks, the meticulous step of scraping off the old paint ensures that only the necessary amount of paint is applied during the restoration process.

It is important to paint the bridge. The bright 'international orange' paint enhances the visibility in fog that develops over the bay area.

This example highlights the significance of balance. Just as the Golden Gate Bridge requires periodic maintenance to sustain its functionality and beauty, we too must assess and shed the unnecessary layers that weigh us down. By embracing minimalism, setting priorities, and seeking partnerships, we can simplify our lives and focus on what truly matters, unlocking our potential to achieve our dreams.

Singapore, a small yet remarkable country, stands as a testament to the possibility of sustainable development. Despite its bustling economic activities and impressive modern infrastructure, Singapore has achieved the remarkable feat of becoming a zero-waste producing nation. This accomplishment showcases the power of a mindful and responsible attitude towards the environment. By prioritizing sustainability and implementing innovative waste management systems, Singapore serves as an inspiring example of how a nation can thrive while simultaneously taking responsibility for its ecological footprint.

We as individuals can be mindful of what all we accumulate in our daily lives on Earth, and in journey of life.

This brings us back to the question we started with, how much are you packing for your journey? How much you want to carry and how far or high you want to go?

Traveling light is an important aspect of minimalistic lifestyle. It is not just about packing fewer items in your suitcase, but about being mindful of what you truly need and what you can do without. By embracing the art of traveling light, you not only simplify your life, but you also equip yourself with the skills and confidence to face adversities and challenges. Whether it be in your personal life or in your professional life, the concept of traveling light can have a profound impact on the way you approach life's journey.

Minimalism can be a powerful tool for personal growth and development. When we shed the excess baggage of our lives, we create space for new experiences, perspectives, and opportunities. By reducing our dependence on material possessions, we free ourselves from the burden of constant upkeep and maintenance. This, in turn, allows us to focus on developing our skills, abilities, and relationships. We become more resilient and better equipped to face life's adversities, with a clearer mind and a lighter spirit.

In business or professional realm, embracing a minimalist lifestyle can bring numerous benefits as well. By simplifying our work processes, we can increase efficiency, reduce stress, and improve overall productivity. By focusing on the essentials, we can make better use of our time, resources, and energy, freeing us up to pursue more meaningful and fulfilling goals.

The new age business trends also reflect something similar, favouring the leaner companies. One example of this concept is the sale of The New York Times to Mexican billionaire Carlos Slim in 1993 for $1.1 billion. Meanwhile, WhatsApp, a much smaller, tech-focused company, was sold to Facebook in 2014 for $19 billion. This contrast demonstrates the value placed on companies that are lean and efficient, utilizing technology to streamline their operations and improve their bottom line. In today's fast-paced business world, the ability to quickly adapt to changing technologies and market conditions is crucial for success, making companies that embrace a minimalist approach more attractive to potential buyers.

Many large corporations have adopted the Lean methodology in recent years, recognizing the benefits it can bring to their operations. By embracing a minimalist approach and continuously seeking out ways to improve, these corporations are able to reduce waste, increase efficiency, and build new capabilities. This allows them to remain competitive and meet the changing demands of the market.

The Lean methodology is not just limited to manufacturing industries. It can be applied to a wide range of sectors, including healthcare, finance, and service industries. By focusing on simplifying processes and eliminating waste, organizations can improve their bottom line and provide better value to their customers. As a result, Lean has become a widely adopted management philosophy in the corporate world, helping organizations of all sizes achieve greater success.

Another great example of a minimalist approach is Elon Musk, a well-known figure in the tech industry, and is known for his bold visions and innovative ideas. One of the most notable examples of his minimalist approach was when he open sourced the Hyperloop project. By recognizing that he would not be able to give the project the attention and resources it needed while also pursuing other big ideas, he chose to hand it over to the open source community. As per Elon musk he wanted to focus on other projects and by giving his Hyperloop idea to open source the best expertise will be available to the project which otherwise would have been limited to his group of companies. And we know that after Hyperloop came to opensource virgin group is one of the first few who actually built infrastructure and hyperloop, in fact they tested things with humans travelling short distances. I am sure by the time you are reading this Virgin and few other companies might already have this operational and running making Elon Musk's idea travelling at 450 Km/h speed.

This decision was a demonstration of his willingness to simplify his priorities and focus on what was truly important to him. By giving up control of the Hyperloop project, Elon Musk was able to redirect his time, resources, and energy towards other ventures that he felt were a higher priority. This type of strategic decision-making is a hallmark of a minimalist approach and is one of the reasons why Elon Musk has been so successful in his career.

The idea behind minimalism is to eliminate distractions and clutter, so that you can focus on what is truly important to you. This can be applied to many aspects of life, from possessions and material goods to time management and personal relationships. When we simplify our lives and focus on what is truly essential, we can create space for growth, creativity, and fulfillment.

In the case of Elon Musk, he was able to simplify his priorities by giving up control of the Hyperloop project. By doing so, he was able to redirect his time, resources, and energy towards other ventures that he felt were a higher priority. This type of strategic decision-making is a hallmark of a minimalist approach and is what sets Elon Musk apart as a successful innovator.

However, it's not always easy to embrace a minimalist lifestyle, especially in a world that's often driven by consumerism and materialism. That's why it's important to be mindful and intentional in our choices, and to be open to the possibility of change. To get started, it may be helpful to reflect on what truly matters to you and what you can do without. This can involve making difficult decisions about what possessions to keep and what to let go of. But it can also involve making changes to our daily routines, habits, and beliefs.

One of the key principles of minimalism is to focus on the essentials. This means prioritizing what's truly important, and letting go of everything else. This can be challenging, but it can also be incredibly freeing. By focusing on the essentials, we can simplify our lives, reduce clutter, and create more time and space for the things that matter most.

In addition to prioritizing what actions to take and what not to take, a minimalist mindset also involves choosing what thoughts to retain and what thoughts not to entertain. Our thoughts have a powerful impact on our actions and ultimately, our results. When we focus on negative and unhelpful thoughts, we can become overwhelmed and stressed, leading to poor decision making and actions that do not align with our values and goals.

To cultivate a minimalist mindset, it is important to choose what thoughts to retain and what thoughts not to entertain. This can involve practicing mindfulness and becoming more aware of our thoughts. When negative or unhelpful thoughts arise, we can choose to let them go and focus instead on positive, constructive thoughts.

In addition, it is important to cultivate a growth mindset and embrace change. By focusing on progress, rather than perfection, we can reduce stress and anxiety and prioritize what truly matters in our lives.

Furthermore, by embracing a minimalist mindset and simplifying our lives, we can reduce distractions and create more time for self-reflection and introspection. This can help us gain a clearer understanding of our values and priorities, and make more intentional choices about what thoughts to retain and what thoughts not to entertain.

Attitude of gratitude

Another important aspect of the minimalist lifestyle is to cultivate a sense of gratitude. Gratitude is a powerful tool that can help cultivate a minimalist mindset. When we cultivate an attitude of gratitude, we shift our focus from what we lack to what we already have. This shift in perspective can help us appreciate what we have and lead to a reduction in the desire to accumulate more possessions.

A minimalist mindset is characterized by a focus on what is truly essential and valuable in life, rather than material possessions. When we are grateful for what we have, we are more likely to prioritize experiences and relationships over things. This leads to a simplification of our lives and a reduction in clutter and excess.

In addition to reducing the desire to accumulate more possessions, gratitude can also lead to a greater sense of contentment and happiness. By focusing on what we have, rather than what we lack, we are more likely to experience a sense of joy and fulfillment in our lives.

Even neuroscience has proven the effect of gratitude on our brains. The UCLA Mindfulness Awareness Research Center says being thankful actually changes our brain structure. It makes us happier. When we appreciate others, it releases the 'good' hormones and keeps our immune system in check.

As per scientists, thanking someone activates the brain's reward center. That alters how we see the world and ourselves.

Dr. Alex Korb, in his book Upward Spiral, says gratitude makes us focus on life's positives.

Our brain focuses on what we have when we say or receive 'thank you' words or messages. It brings intrinsic motivation and strong awareness. At the neurochemical level, gratitude sparks neurotransmitters like serotonin and dopamine, managing our emotions and stress.

That is why I say, it's important to be mindful of our relationships. By developing strong and supportive relationships with others, we can build a network of support that will help us navigate the ups and downs of life. This can include leveraging our strengths and seeking out the help of others when we need it, as well as offering support and encouragement to those around us.

Life will always bring its own set of challenges, but it is how we respond to these challenges that defines us. The bigger the challenges we face, the more we have grown and evolved as individuals. However, it can be easy to get bogged down by adversity, to feel overwhelmed and defeated. But we must remember that the first step in overcoming these challenges is to simplify our lives and shed the excess baggage that holds us back. Be it physical, mental, or emotional clutter. Once we get rid of that it gives way to clarity in life.

Empty Your Bags. Unlock Your Potential.

Embracing minimalism and simplifying our lives can bring great benefits. By shedding distractions and focusing on what truly matters, we can approach challenges with a clear mind and purpose. To achieve this, we must cultivate our own abilities, embrace change, and continually strive for growth and improvement. Just like Buddhist monks who can meditate in extreme cold, we too can develop resilience to life's adversities.

As we grow, it's important to also build strong relationships through effective communication. This helps us reach new heights and achieve our goals, making the most of the opportunities that life presents. So, let's embrace minimalism, focus on the essentials, and continuously develop ourselves, both physically and mentally, to live a fulfilling and limitless life.

Nature provides us with countless examples of creatures who have developed the ability to adjust to adverse conditions, such as bioluminescence in deep-sea creatures. These organisms have learned to produce their own light, allowing them to survive and thrive in environments where there is no sun. As humans, we are even more fortunate, as we have access to the best that nature has to offer. Let us make the most of this opportunity and embrace our own limitless potential.

Ajay Rawat

What's your excuse?

Travelling light is not just about packing light, it's also about adopting a minimalist mindset towards life. The idea is not to get bogged down by material possessions and to focus on experiences and personal growth instead. This philosophy has been practiced by many individuals throughout history, from early humans who roamed the earth with very little, to modern-day minimalists who live with only the essentials.

The key to this philosophy is to not let a lack of resources hold you back from pursuing your dreams and goals. Many people use their lack of resources as an excuse for not moving forward, but the truth is that we often have more than we need to get started. By finding creative solutions and looking for alternative ways to accomplish our goals, we can break free from the limitations of our current situation and achieve great things.

Taking a leap of faith and stepping outside of our comfort zone can be daunting, but it's often necessary for growth and success. By letting go of our attachments to material possessions and embracing the unknown, we can find new opportunities and experiences that we may have never thought possible.

In essence, the message behind **travelling light is about living a fulfilling and purposeful life, regardless of our resources or circumstances.** It's about focusing on the journey rather than the destination, and being open to new experiences and opportunities along the way. So, ask yourself, what's stopping you from taking that leap of faith and embarking on your own personal journey?

Kyle Maynard's accomplishment of climbing Mount Kilimanjaro and Mount Aconcagua without prosthetic limbs is truly remarkable. Born with congenital amputation, Kyle has no arms or legs, which makes even simple tasks, such as getting dressed, challenging for him. However, he has never let his physical disability hold him back from pursuing his dreams.

To climb Mount Kilimanjaro, Kyle relied on his incredible upper body strength and a specially designed wheelchair. He spent nearly ten days climbing the mountain, crawling on his hands and knees for much of the way. He also used a custom-made prosthetic device that allowed him to climb steep inclines and navigate rocky terrain. Despite encountering numerous obstacles along the way, including altitude sickness and harsh weather conditions, Kyle remained determined to reach the summit.

Kyle's climb of Mount Aconcagua was an even greater challenge. At 22,841 feet, it is the highest peak in South America, and the climb took Kyle nearly a month to complete. He had to crawl for most of the journey, using his arms and hands to pull himself up the mountain. The terrain was treacherous, with steep inclines, loose rocks, and deep snow drifts, but Kyle persevered, driven by his desire to achieve this incredible feat.

Kyle's climbing achievements are a testament to his incredible physical and mental strength, as well as his determination to overcome the challenges that come with his disability. He has inspired countless others to push past their own limitations and pursue their dreams, no matter how impossible they may seem.

Often, people assume that certain physical or mental disabilities make it impossible to pursue certain goals or passions. However, as the examples I mentioned earlier demonstrate, there are many ways to overcome these challenges and achieve great things.

It's important to remember that resources and tools are available to help individuals with disabilities pursue their dreams. Assistive technology, adaptive equipment, and other resources can make it possible to participate in activities that might otherwise seem out of reach.

But even more important than resources or equipment is a positive mindset and a willingness to persevere in the face of challenges. The human spirit is capable of amazing things, and with determination and resilience, anything is possible.

So, if you have a dream or a passion that seems out of reach because of a physical or mental disability, don't give up! Explore the resources and tools available to you, and focus on developing a positive mindset and a can-do attitude. With hard work and dedication, you can achieve amazing things and inspire others to do the same.

Empty Your Bags. Unlock Your Potential.

Drawing from my personal experience, I once traveled between two cities that were more than 1500 kilometres apart with just 12 dollars not in my pocket, but in my bank account. Although it might sound crazy to undertake such a journey with so little money, it turned out to be an amazing adventure.

Vivekananda, the great Indian monk and philosopher, is known to have travelled with very limited belongings when he set out to travel around the world. According to historical accounts, he only took a few basic essentials with him, including a saffron-colored robe, a pair of sandals, and a water pot. This minimalist approach to travel was in line with his spiritual beliefs, as he believed that material possessions were a hindrance to the journey of self-discovery and enlightenment.

Vivekananda's minimalist approach to travel was also a practical choice, as it allowed him to move freely and easily from place to place. This was especially important for him, as he was on a mission to spread the teachings of Hinduism and spirituality to the Western world. By traveling light, he was able to focus all his energy and resources on his mission, rather than being weighed down by excess baggage.

In this sense, Vivekananda's approach to travel is a lesson for us all. It shows us that by simplifying our lives and focusing on what is truly important, we can achieve more and have a more fulfilling experience, both on our physical journeys and on our journey of life. By embracing the idea of traveling light, we can learn to prioritize what is truly important and pursue our goals and dreams with confidence and clarity.

There is another story from India. The story of the Indian artist, Pradyumna Kumar Mahanandia, also known as PK, and his journey to meet his Swedish love, Charlotte Von Schedvin, is one of the most romantic and inspiring stories of all time.

PK, who was born into a poor family in a small village in eastern India, had a talent for drawing from a very young age. Despite his financial struggles, he managed to pursue his passion for art and eventually became a successful artist in his hometown of New Delhi.

In 1975, PK met Charlotte, a young Swedish girl, who was visiting India. They fell in love, but Charlotte had to return to Sweden. They promised to keep in touch, but in those days, communication was limited to letters, which took weeks to arrive.

Determined to be reunited with Charlotte, PK decided to embark on an epic journey. He sold all his possessions, including his beloved art supplies, and bought a bicycle. With only a few rupees in his pocket, he began his journey across Asia and Europe, covering over 7,000 miles.

For four months, PK rode through the rugged terrain, facing extreme weather conditions, language barriers,

Empty Your Bags. Unlock Your Potential.

and various other challenges. He often slept on the side of the road or in cheap hotels, but he never gave up on his mission.

Finally, he arrived in Sweden, exhausted and hungry, but filled with hope and excitement to see Charlotte again. When they finally reunited, it was a beautiful moment that captured the hearts of people all over the world.

PK and Charlotte eventually got married and started a life together in Sweden. PK continued his career as an artist and became famous for his portrait paintings. He also wrote a book about his incredible journey, titled "The Amazing Story of the Man Who Cycled from India to Europe for Love."

Let PK's, Vivekananda's, and Kyle Maynard's incredible story be a source of inspiration for all of us. Let it remind us that we should never let obstacles or limitations deter us from following our hearts and chasing our dreams. By traveling light, both in our physical journeys and in life, we can focus on what truly matters and create our own extraordinary stories. Embrace the spirit of adventure, and let your dreams take flight. The world is waiting for you.

Empty Your Bags. Unlock Your Potential.

Ajay Rawat

Arrival

Empty Your Bags. Unlock Your Potential.

Seeds and weeds

When you go on a hike, you may notice that certain things like cleavers, catch weeds, and sticky willies stick to your clothes, hair, and gear as you venture along the trail. These things can be either weeds or seeds. These stick to your clothes and hair without your knowledge. I don't think anybody would get them intentionally. I don't think anybody plans their treks or hikes specially to get these catch weeds and sticky willies, unless they are studying or researching these plants.

These unwanted weeds can be prickly plants, burrs, or other natural things that attach themselves to your clothes, shoes, and gear, making it hard for you to move freely and comfortably or causing irritation, rashes, or itching on your skin, which can ruin your trekking experience or even cause some health issues.

Weeds can also represent unwanted negative thoughts, emotions, and habits that weigh you down and make it challenging to move forward in life and impact your overall life experiences.

However, not everything that sticks to you during your hike is a hindrance. Seeds can also find their way onto your clothes and gear, or you might pick them intentionally at times. These seeds can be the beginnings of new plants, trees, or other natural elements. They can be carried by the wind, animals, or water, and when they find a suitable spot, they take root and grow into something beautiful and vibrant.

Similarly, in life, seeds represent new opportunities, ideas, relationships, and experiences. They have the potential to bring growth and positive change. Just like the seeds that stick to your clothes during a hike, these opportunities may come unexpectedly, carried by the winds of chance or presented to you by the people and circumstances you encounter.

It's crucial to be mindful of both the weeds and the seeds that come into your life. Weeds can multiply quickly, entangling you in negative patterns, destructive relationships, and self-limiting beliefs. If left unaddressed, they can hinder your personal growth and prevent you from reaching your full potential.

On the other hand, seeds are the gems of possibility and potential. They have the power to transform your life if nurtured and given the chance to grow. By recognizing and embracing the seeds that come your way, you open yourself up to new adventures, personal development, and meaningful connections.

Trekking can be a metaphor for life, where you encounter both weeds and seeds along the way. The key is to be mindful of what you allow into your life and to take steps to remove the weeds and nurture the seeds that can help you grow and thrive.

To navigate this metaphorical journey, it's essential to take control of what you allow to fill your metaphorical bags. When you don't exercise your power of choice,

Empty Your Bags. Unlock Your Potential.

these bags can quickly become filled with things, memories, habits, emotions, and feelings that weigh you down. They can hinder your progress and make even the simplest tasks feel like distant dreams.

However, by actively choosing what to fill your bags with, you regain control over your journey. You have the power to decide what you want to carry with you on your life's path. You can choose to fill your mind with dreams, aspirations, and positive thoughts that propel you forward.

Remember, the power to choose is always there and it is within you. It is through conscious choices that you shape your journey, fill your bags, and create a life that aligns with your dreams and aspirations. Take ownership of what you allow into your life and let go of anything that no longer serves you.

By exercising your power to choose, you become the architect of your journey, the curator of your experiences, and the author of your story. Embrace this power, and with each deliberate choice, you pave the way for a more fulfilling, meaningful, and joyous life journey.

These six empty bags that we have been talking about are waiting to be filled. Like when I picked my ruck sack after all the planning and deliberation I could only fill it to 60 % of its capacity in the planning stage, but I ended up filling it to 125% of capacity. I only know, how I managed to close it. Same way, if you do not choose what fills those bags, they will be filled with anything and everything that comes your way. Without conscious decision-making, the bags will quickly accumulate excess baggage, weighing you down and hindering your progress.

The accumulation of unnecessary items and burdens can happen so subtly and swiftly that you may not even realize it until you find yourself struggling to move forward. The excess baggage becomes a barrier, preventing you from embracing simpler and easier things in life. Your dreams and aspirations may feel out of reach, as the weight of the baggage limits your ability to imagine and believe in what is possible.

Furthermore, when your bags are filled with unwanted and disempowering notions, they can sap your energies and leave you feeling stuck and unmotivated. These fixed beliefs and negative perspectives not only impact you but also have a ripple effect on your immediate family, close friends, workplaces, and society as a whole.

When you carry the baggage of negative thoughts, it can influence your relationships, leading to strained connections and a lack of fulfillment in your interactions. It can hinder your performance and growth in your work environments, preventing you from reaching your full potential and making a meaningful impact. On a larger scale, the baggage you carry can contribute to a culture of limitations and complacency within society, hindering progress and innovation.

However, when you exercise your power to choose, you reclaim control over what fills your bags. You have the opportunity to select what aligns with your values, passions, and aspirations. By intentionally choosing what you allow into your life, you create space for empowering beliefs, positive energy, and meaningful experiences.

By consciously choosing the contents of your bags, you can let go of the excess items that no longer serves you. This act of release liberates you from the weight that holds you back, allowing you to move forward with more ease, clarity, and purpose. As you lighten your load, you open yourself up to new possibilities, enabling you to imagine and dream freely once again.

Not only will this positively impact your own journey, but it will also radiate outwards, influencing those around you. By embodying the power of choice and embracing a mindset of empowerment, you inspire others to do the same. Your actions become a catalyst for transformation, creating a ripple effect of growth, positivity, and limitless potential within your immediate sphere of influence and beyond.

Remember, the power to choose what fills your bags lies within you, and by exercising this power, you can embark on a transformative journey of self-discovery and personal growth.

Ajay Rawat

Your bags and YOU

Six empty bags. Carry your six empty bags. Have you been wondering why it would be necessary to empty these six bags when they will simply be filled up again? With the power to make my own decisions, what is the purpose of me carrying around these six bags with nothing inside them? As we often have to empty the items eventually, why bother to keep 'carrying' them?

Well, it is natural to have these questions.

The answer is, you can't get rid of these bags. Because these bags are not separate from you. These six bags are not separate entities that can be discarded or abandoned. They are an integral part of who you are as an individual. These bags represent your thoughts, knowledge, actions, emotions, and imagination – the very essence of your being.

You see, the bags we carry are not merely physical objects, but symbolic representations of our inner world. They are containers that hold the treasures and burdens of our experiences. They are reflections of our thoughts, beliefs, and attitudes. They are manifestations of our choices and the consequences they bring. They are reflection of choices you make and actions you take.

Empty Your Bags. Unlock Your Potential.

When we acknowledge that these bags are interconnected with our identity, we realize the significance of what we choose to fill them with. Every thought we entertain, every piece of knowledge we acquire, every action we take, every emotion we experience, and every dream we dare to imagine contributes to the contents of these bags. They shape our perspectives, shape our behaviors, and shape the trajectory of our lives.

Therefore, it becomes imperative to exercise conscious control over what we allow to occupy these bags. When we recognize the power within us to determine their contents, we become aware of the impact our choices have on our overall well-being and the lives of those around us.

By deliberately choosing to fill our bags with positivity, knowledge, empathy, and passion, we transform ourselves into individuals who radiate love, compassion, and inspiration. We become beacons of light in a world that often feels consumed by darkness. Our bags become vessels of hope, wisdom, and creativity that uplift not only ourselves but also those we encounter on our journey.

On the other hand, if we passively allow our bags to be filled with negativity, ignorance, apathy, and fear, we risk becoming burdened by the weight of our own choices. These bags can become a source of self-imposed limitations, inhibiting our growth and preventing us from reaching our full potential. They can constrain our ability to empathize, to understand, and to connect with others. They can stifle our dreams and confine us to a life of mediocrity.

But the power lies within us to consciously shape the contents of these bags. It is through our awareness, intention, and commitment that we can select what aligns with our values, what nourishes our souls, and what propels us toward personal and collective growth.

You have the power

In addition to being aware of the weeds and seeds that come into your life, it's crucial to recognize your power to choose. You have the ability to decide what you want to pick up and what you want to let go of along your journey.

Imagine your six empty bags as blank canvases waiting to be filled with the elements that align with your values, passions, and aspirations. Take a moment to reflect on what truly matters to you and what you want to prioritize in your life.

When it comes to your mind, exercise your power to choose empowering thoughts over self-limiting ones. Replace doubts and fears with affirmations and positive self-talk. Embrace a growth mindset that believes in your ability to learn, improve, and overcome obstacles.

Knowledge is a valuable asset that you can choose to accumulate. Seek out learning opportunities that resonate with your interests and goals. Expand your horizons through reading, attending workshops, taking courses, or engaging in meaningful conversations. Fill your bag of knowledge with the tools and insights that will support your personal and professional development.

Time is a finite resource, and how you choose to spend it has a profound impact on your journey. Be intentional with your time and set priorities that align with your values. Evaluate your commitments and eliminate those that no longer serve you. Make space for activities and relationships that bring you joy, fulfillment, and personal growth.

Your heart is a powerful compass in your journey. Choose to fill it with love, compassion, and kindness. Nurture meaningful relationships and surround yourself with people who uplift and inspire you. Let go of toxic connections that drain your energy and hinder your progress. Create space in your heart for genuine connections that bring joy, support, and a sense of belonging.

Habits are the building blocks of your life. Take charge of your habits by consciously choosing ones that align with your goals and values. Identify habits that no longer serve you and replace them with positive ones. Whether it's practicing mindfulness, maintaining a healthy lifestyle, or cultivating a habit of gratitude, choose habits that contribute to your overall well-being and personal growth.

Lastly, your know-how is a powerful tool for shaping your journey. Embrace your curiosity and the desire to learn and explore. Allow yourself to dream and imagine a life filled with possibilities. Continuously expand your know-how by seeking new experiences, acquiring new skills, and staying open to lifelong learning. By doing so, you empower yourself to navigate challenges, seize opportunities, and evolve into the best version of yourself.

Remember, the power to choose is within you. It is through conscious choices that you shape your journey, fill your bags, and create a life that aligns with your dreams and aspirations. Take ownership of what you allow into your life and let go of anything that no longer serves you.

As you reflect on the significance of these bags, remember that they are not burdens to be cast aside but vessels of opportunity and transformation. Embrace the responsibility and privilege of curating their contents with purpose, joy, and authenticity.

Carry your bags with pride, knowing that each one holds the potential to contribute to a more compassionate, enlightened, and harmonious world. Embrace the journey of life as an ongoing process of filling, emptying, and refining these bags, for it is through this conscious engagement that we cultivate our truest selves and leave a lasting legacy.

Yes, you have the power and control to shape your own journey in life by consciously selecting what you fill in your six bags. Each bag presents an opportunity for you to create, recreate, discover, rediscover, imagine, and reimagine yourself.

Consider these bags as canvases awaiting your unique expression. You have the freedom to paint them with vibrant colors, intricate details, and inspiring visions. It is within your grasp to fill them with dreams that ignite your passion, knowledge that expands your horizons, actions that align with your values, emotions that uplift your spirit, and imaginings that transcend the boundaries of what is known.

In this ever-evolving journey, you are not confined to a static identity or fixed trajectory. Instead, you have the privilege of continuously shaping and reshaping who you are, shedding old beliefs and embracing new perspectives. With each passing moment, you have the opportunity to refine the contents of your bags, discarding what no longer serves you and welcoming what enriches your soul.

Do not underestimate the transformative power of choice. By consciously curating the contents of your bags, you become an active participant in your own growth and self-discovery. You have the ability to shed self-imposed limitations, challenge societal norms, and defy the boundaries that hold you back.

Embrace the fluidity of your journey and the endless possibilities that lie before you. Take delight in the process of exploration, as you navigate the landscapes of your mind, heart, and soul. Allow yourself the freedom to evolve, to learn, and to unlearn. With each new experience and every intentional choice, you are sculpting the masterpiece of your life.

And remember, this power to choose and shape your journey extends far beyond your individual existence. Your influence has a ripple effect that touches the lives

Empty Your Bags. Unlock Your Potential.

of those around you. By consciously filling your bags with love, kindness, and authenticity, you inspire and uplift others on their own paths of self-discovery.

So, my friend, embrace the power within you. Embrace the opportunity to create, recreate, discover, rediscover, imagine, and reimagine yourself. Your journey is a constant invitation to evolve, to transcend limitations, and to embrace the fullness of your potential. May your bags be filled with the essence of your truest self, and may your journey be one of endless growth, joy, and fulfillment.

After reading this book, you have learned the importance of emptying your bags in life. By emptying your mind, knowledge, time, heart, habits, and know-hows, you can experience a fulfilling and meaningful life. It is essential to understand that carrying an empty bag means making space for new experiences, skills, and knowledge to enter your life. Your journey in life will be more enriching and inspiring when you embrace the concept of emptying your bags regularly.

As you embark on your journey, I encourage you to carry six empty bags with you. Carry an empty bag of the mind to carry more dreams and decisions. With an empty bag of knowledge, you can learn new beautiful things, develop new skills, and gather new knowledge. An empty bag of time allows you to experience freedom and create timeless memories for life.

Carrying an empty bag of heart allows you to make new connections with authenticity. An empty bag of habits enables you to give up old regressive and disempowering habits, making space for new empowering ones. Finally, an empty bag of know-how gives you the freedom to dream more and dream with freedom.

Always remember that every single step you take in a new direction opens a million new portals of possibilities for you. So, keep your bags empty and open to new experiences, knowledge, and opportunities. The journey of life is a never-ending process of learning, growing, and evolving. The more you empty your bags, the more you can fill them with meaningful experiences that bring joy and fulfillment to your life.

Empty Your Bags. Unlock Your Potential.

How much do you pack?

So, what all and how much do you pack for your travel? The answer to this question is ultimately up to you, completely your choice. But as we reach the end of "Empty Your Bags and Unlock Your Potential," I encourage you to consider the power of embracing a minimalistic lifestyle, prioritization, and partnership. These concepts can transform the way you approach your journey, enabling you to travel lighter and more confidently, no matter where life takes you. Just as we carefully select the essential items for our physical travels, we can apply the same principles to our inner journey of the mind and spirit.

We make room for what truly matters by letting go of needless baggage, both physical and emotional. We can choose and focus on our true passions and objectives by prioritising them, directing our efforts towards achieving them. And as we form alliances with like-minded people, we discover the power and support that comes from being in touch with those who share our hopes and goals.

Remember, the universe exists with us, within us, and for us. It is a vast reservoir of endless opportunities waiting to be explored. The Sanskrit phrase "Aham Brahmasmi," meaning "I am the universe," encapsulates the profound truth that we are interconnected with the cosmic forces that surround us.

So, dear reader, as you embark on your unique journey, I invite you to travel light, both in the physical realm and within your inner self. Simplify your life, focus on what is truly important, and achieve more with less. Embrace the vastness of the universe, allow it to inspire and empower you, and know that you can achieve anything you can imagine or dream of. The universe is there to support you, offering endless possibilities and opportunities for growth and fulfillment. With these tools and concepts in your possession, your potential is truly limitless.

Empty Your Bags. Unlock Your Potential.

Ajay Rawat

*Are you stepping out with your
six empty bags
on your next journey?*

Empty Your Bags. Unlock Your Potential.

Ajay Rawat

Glossary

11	High-altitude trek	Here it is referred to a challenging outdoor adventure involving hiking or walking at elevations of 4000 meters above sea level.
14	Hedonic treadmill	A psychological theory that suggests people return to a baseline level of happiness despite major positive or negative life events
24	Five Whys or Three Whys.	The "Five Whys" is a problem-solving method using iterative questioning, asking "Why?" five times to identify the root cause of an issue. It's widely used in business and manufacturing.
		The "Three Whys" is a simplified version, involving three iterations of asking "Why?" to explore deeper causes. Both aim to uncover fundamental issues and

Empty Your Bags. Unlock Your Potential.

		address root causes in problem-solving.
43	Analysis Paralysis	A situation where overthinking or excessive data analysis hinders decision-making, causing delays or inaction due to an abundance of information or choices
46	Blue sky thinking	Thinking without constraints or limitations, often used to encourage creative, open-minded, and innovative brainstorming
54	gTum Mo	A form of Tibetan Buddhist meditation practice
90	Dopamin	A neurotransmitter, a brain chemical that acts like a reward signal, making you feel good when you achieve something or experience pleasure
91	Prefrontal cortex	Brain's front region, involved in decision-making, personality, and moderating social behavior. It's like your brain's CEO

94	Multiple Trace Theory (MTT)	Multiple Trace Theory (MTT) is a memory consolidation model advanced by Lynn Nadel and colleagues, as an alternative to the "standard model" of memory consolidation. In this model, hippocampus is always involved in storage and retrieval of episodic memory, but semantic memory can be established in neocortex.
95	Hippocampus	Brain structure associated with memory and learning
95	Amygdala	A brain region responsible for processing emotions, particularly fear and anxiety. Think of it as your emotional alarm system
97	Cortisol	A hormone your body makes when you're stressed. It's like your internal stress alarm, preparing you for challenges.
108	Hierarchy of needs	A psychological theory by Abraham Maslow, explaining human motivation. It arranges

		needs in a pyramid, from basic necessities like food and shelter to higher-level goals like self-actualization
110	Pareto principle	The Pareto Principle, or the 80/20 rule, suggests that roughly 80% of results come from 20% of causes. It's used to highlight the unequal distribution of outcomes in various situations.
112	Stoicism	Stoicism is a philosophical system that emphasizes rationality, virtue, and emotional resilience. It encourages individuals to accept what they cannot control, prioritize moral goodness, and find inner tranquility by aligning their actions and thoughts with these principles.
112	Ataraxia	A pleasure that comes when the mind is at rest
115	Brahmacharya	Brahmacharya Ashram is the first stage of life in Hindu philosophy's four-stage system. It represents the

		student phase, focusing on education and religious training to build a foundation for spiritual practice. While traditionally associated with celibacy, it can also mean self-restraint and moderation, especially in contemporary times, as individuals prepare for later life stages.
115	Grihastha	The Grihastha Ashram is the second stage in Hindu philosophy's four-stage system. It's known as the "householder" stage, where individuals typically establish families, maintain homes, and pursue both material success (artha) and pleasures (kama) while upholding ethical principles (dharma). This stage emphasizes being supportive family members and productive contributors to society.
116	Vanaprastha	The Vanaprastha Ashram is the third stage in Hindu philosophy's four-stage system. Traditionally, it involved individuals detaching

Empty Your Bags. Unlock Your Potential.

from family life and material pursuits to devote more time to spiritual practice. While some may still retreat to forests, modern practitioners often focus on giving back to their communities, volunteering, reading scriptures, and deepening their spiritual journey. The goal is selfless service (seva) and the pursuit of spiritual liberation (moksha).

| 116 | Sannyasa | The Sannyasa Ashram, the fourth stage in Hindu philosophy's four-stage system, involves renunciation. Some enter it at a young age, dedicating their lives to scriptural study and a monastic lifestyle, while others transition to it later in life after fulfilling prior obligations. Sannyasins live simply, with minimal possessions, and are committed to nonviolence. Their ultimate goal is liberation from the cycle of birth and rebirth (moksha). |

116	Lean Startup methodology	The Lean Startup methodology is an approach for developing businesses and products that emphasizes iterative development, continuous testing, and efficient use of resources to build and scale ventures more effectively.
117	Minimum viable product	A Minimum Viable Product (MVP) is the simplest version of a product with enough features to satisfy early customers and gain feedback for further development, typically used in the Lean Startup approach.
121	Leverage	Strategic use of resources, influence, or advantage to amplify or maximize the desired outcome or impact in various contexts, such as business, relationships, or problem-solving, often by exploiting available opportunities or assets effectively.

122	Equilibrium of Planes	Equilibrium of Planes, as understood by Archimedes, denotes a state where forces on a flat surface are balanced, a concept crucial in his study of statics, ensuring both translational and rotational stability
122	Archimedes screw	The Archimedes screw is one of the earliest documented forms of a screw-like device, and it dates back to ancient Greece, attributed to the mathematician and inventor Archimedes in the 3rd century BCE. While it's among the early screw inventions, it's not definitively the very first, as the historical record might not capture all ancient innovations.
122	Claw of Archimedes	The Claw of Archimedes is a historic weapon designed by Archimedes to defend against naval attacks. It consisted of a large crane-like device with a clawed grappling hook used to lift and capsize enemy ships.

124	Tao Te Ching	The "Tao Te Ching" is a foundational Chinese philosophical text attributed to Laozi, offering insights into Taoism. It explores the concept of the Tao (the Way) and imparts wisdom on living in harmony with it.
124	Wu-wei	Wu-wei is a Chinese Taoist concept that translates to "non-action" or "effortless action." It advocates for natural, spontaneous, and unforced behavior, aligning with the flow of the Tao (the Way). Wu-wei encourages individuals to act without striving, allowing events to unfold naturally, and achieving harmony with the world.
126	Law of karma	The law of karma is a spiritual belief in which a person's actions and intentions have consequences, influencing their future experiences and circumstances, whether in this life or future reincarnations.

142   The Five Love Languages

"The Five Love Languages" is a concept developed by Dr. Gary Chapman in his book of the same name. It identifies five primary ways people express and receive love:

1. Words of Affirmation: Expressing love through verbal compliments and affirmations.
2. Acts of Service: Demonstrating love by doing helpful tasks or acts of service.
3. Receiving Gifts: Feeling loved through thoughtful gift-giving.
4. Quality Time: Experiencing love by spending focused and quality time together.
5. Physical Touch: Feeling loved through physical affection like hugs, kisses, and cuddling.

The idea is that people have a dominant love language, and understanding and using each other's love languages can enhance relationships.

144	Sherpas	Sherpas historically lived in the mountainous regions of Nepal and Tibet, where they have settled villages and communities at high altitudes. They are known for their mountain-based lifestyle, including agriculture and guiding climbers, rather than a nomadic way of life characterized by constant movement.
158	Saam, daam, dand, bhed	"Saam, daam, dand, bhed" is a Hindi phrase that describes four different strategies or approaches often used to achieve a goal or resolve a problem:

1. Saam: Persuasion through discussion and reasoning, seeking a peaceful resolution.
2. Daam: Achieving the goal through material incentives or negotiation, typically involving some form of compromise.
3. Dand: Using punishment or force to attain the objective.
4. Bhed: Employing division or manipulation to create

discord or confusion among opponents to gain an advantage.

These strategies are often associated with political or strategic decision-making.

166	Intrinsic motivation	Intrinsic motivation refers to the internal drive or personal desire that leads individuals to engage in an activity for the inherent satisfaction, enjoyment, or interest it provides, rather than for external rewards or pressures.
166	Extrinsic motivation	Extrinsic motivation is the drive to engage in an activity based on external rewards, such as money, praise, or recognition, rather than personal enjoyment or inherent interest in the activity itself.
180	Cognitive dissonance	**Cognitive dissonance** is the mental stress or discomfort experienced by an individual who holds two or more contradictory beliefs,

		ideas, or values at the same time, or is confronted by new information that conflicts with existing beliefs, ideas, or values.
203	The book of Ecclesiastes	The Book of Ecclesiastes is a biblical text in the Old Testament that explores themes of wisdom, meaning, and the fleeting nature of human life, often attributed to King Solomon.
204	Old Testament	The Old Testament is the first section of the Christian Bible, containing religious texts and scriptures of Judaism and early Christianity, primarily composed before the birth of Jesus Christ.
218	Red Bull's Stratos jump	Red Bull's Stratos jump was a record-breaking space dive in 2012 when Felix Baumgartner parachuted from the stratosphere to Earth's surface.
222	Renaissance	The Renaissance, a transformative cultural and intellectual movement from the 14th to 17th centuries,

Empty Your Bags. Unlock Your Potential.

		revived classical learning, emphasizing art, literature, science, and humanism. It marked a profound shift from medieval traditions, influencing Europe's cultural, social, and scientific landscape.
229	Neuro-Linguistic Programming (NLP)	Neuro-Linguistic Programming (NLP) is a psychological approach that examines the connections between thoughts, language, and behaviors, with the goal of improving communication, personal development, and therapy techniques.
247	Great Pacific Garbage Patch	The Great Pacific Garbage Patch is a massive area in the North Pacific Ocean where marine debris, primarily plastic waste, accumulates due to ocean currents.
248	Bioaccumulation	Bioaccumulation is the process by which harmful substances, such as toxins or pollutants, accumulate and increase in concentration within the tissues of organisms as they

		consume contaminated food or water.
249	Project Kaisei	Project Kaisei is an initiative aimed at researching and addressing plastic pollution in the oceans, particularly focusing on the Great Pacific Garbage Patch.
249	The Ocean Cleanup Project	The Ocean Cleanup Project is an organization that develops technologies to remove plastic waste and debris from the world's oceans, with a mission to clean up plastic pollution.
251	Passivation	Passivation is a chemical process that forms a protective layer on a metal surface to prevent corrosion or chemical reactions.
252	ClearSpace SA	ClearSpace SA is a Swiss startup and a space debris removal company aiming to clean up space by capturing and removing defunct satellites and debris.
252	Golden Gate Bridge	The Golden Gate Bridge is an iconic suspension bridge

		located in San Francisco, California, spanning the Golden Gate Strait.
256	Hyperloop project	The Hyperloop project is an experimental transportation concept involving high-speed travel in low-pressure tubes, initially proposed by Elon Musk.
264	Mount Kilimanjaro	Africa's highest peak, part of the Seven Summits challenge, and a UNESCO World Heritage site, drawing climbers worldwide.
264	Mount Aconcagua	Mount Aconcagua is the highest peak outside Asia, a part of the Seven Summits challenge, and a renowned mountaineering destination.
272	Sticky willies	"Sticky willies" are plants or seeds with hook-like structures that adhere to surfaces, aiding in seed dispersal by attaching to animals or clothing.
287	Aham Brahmasmi	"Aham Brahmasmi" is a Sanskrit phrase from Hindu philosophy, one of the four

Mahavakyas (great sayings) in Vedantic texts. It means "I am Brahm" or "I am the Ultimate Reality." It signifies the realization that one's true self (Atman) is identical to the ultimate reality (Brah), highlighting the unity of the individual soul with the divine.

Empty Your Bags. Unlock Your Potential.

Acknowledgement

I am deeply honored and privileged to write a few words of acknowledgment for the extraordinary individuals who have been a constant source of support throughout the remarkable journey of writing my first book, "Empty your bags. Unlock your potential."

These exceptional individuals have played an indispensable role in fueling my passion and providing untiring encouragement. Their belief in my abilities have served as an endless source of motivation, propelling me forward on this transformative writing expedition.

First and foremost, I am incredibly grateful to **Tony Robbins** and **Arfeen Khan** for their exceptional coaching and invaluable guidance, which has been at the source of this book. Their profound insights and wisdom have instilled in me the courage to surpass the limitations I once believed in.

Under their mentorship, I found the inspiration and motivation to take action beyond my self-imposed boundaries. It was during their respective transformative trainings that I not only started but also successfully completed the journey of writing this book.

Empty Your Bags. Unlock Your Potential.

As a person who always identified myself as a visual person, focused on my professional expertise as a Creative Director in graphic design, the idea of writing a book seemed far-fetched. However, Tony Robbins and Arfeen Khan's guidance pushed me to explore and embrace new avenues of self-expression.

Their distinct coaching provided me with the tools and mindset necessary to transcend my own limiting beliefs. They helped me recognize that my potential extended beyond my established professional identity, empowering me to venture into uncharted territories.

Through their unwavering support and belief in my abilities, I was able to break free from my self-imposed constraints and unlock a dormant passion for writing. This book marks a significant milestone as my first-ever written work, a testament to the transformative power of their coaching.

I am forever grateful to Tony Robbins and Arfeen Khan for their profound impact on my life and for helping me discover and nurture this newfound passion for writing. Their coaching has broadened my horizons, proving that I am capable of much more than I had ever imagined.

While I had the privilege of receiving separate trainings from Tony Robbins and Arfeen Khan, it is important to acknowledge that my journey of transformation started decades ago. It was during those formative years that I was introduced to trainings inspired by Werner Erhard's coaching, which profoundly transformed my thought process and approach towards life.

The impact of those earlier trainings cannot be overstated. They provided me with a framework for personal growth, self-discovery, and a shift in perspective that has influenced every aspect of my life, including the writing of this book.

These trainings exposed me to new ways of thinking, challenging my beliefs and assumptions about what was possible. They equipped me with tools to navigate life's challenges, expand my potential, and embrace a more empowered mindset.

The teachings based on **Werner Erhard's** coaching shaped the very core of my being, influencing my approach to personal and professional development. They fostered a deep sense of self-awareness and instilled in me a commitment to continuous growth and learning.

It would require an entire book to do justice to the depth and breadth of their influence. Each training held valuable lessons and insights that have shaped my path and contributed to the creation of this book.

This book would not have been possible without the incredible contributions of the coaches and trainers who have shared their knowledge and expertise with me. I am truly grateful for their generosity and willingness to share their best practices and methodologies. Their guidance and support have been invaluable in helping me achieve my goals, and I am truly grateful for their unshakable belief in me.

Their wisdom has been instrumental in shaping the soul of this book, and I hope that readers will benefit from their insights as much as I have.

I would also like to thank my fellow seekers who have generously shared their stories and experiences with me. I offer my sincerest thanks for your willingness to open up and be vulnerable, as your courage has been a wellspring of inspiration for me.

Your stories have had a profound impact on my personal journey of learning and growth. They have provided me with valuable insights, different perspectives, and a deeper understanding of the human experience. Your willingness to share both triumphs and challenges has reminded me of the power of resilience, determination, and the capacity for transformation.

I am truly grateful for the inspiration I have drawn from your journeys. Your stories have encouraged me to push beyond my limits, embrace new possibilities, and continue evolving as a person. Your authenticity and vulnerability have served as a reminder that we are all connected by our shared experiences and the universal desire for personal growth and fulfillment.

As I present these stories within the pages of this book, my hope is that readers will also find them inspiring and motivating. I aspire for these narratives to resonate with others on their own paths of self-discovery and empower them to embrace their potential. Your willingness to share has made it possible for me to weave a tapestry of diverse experiences that can touch the hearts and minds of those who read these words.

I am also grateful to my friends at work who introduced me to the world of training programs and resources. Their guidance, support, partnerships, and willingness to think differently have been invaluable in expanding my horizons and deepening my understanding. I am truly fortunate to have such extraordinary individuals by my side, enriching my journey of transformation and professional excellence.

I am deeply grateful for the countless individuals who have supported and encouraged me along the way. Your belief in me has been a constant source of strength and motivation, and I am truly fortunate to have such amazing friends in my life.

In addition, there are some special group of friends, mentors, guides, and teachers who specifically supported in some or other form to make this book a reality. Their input, feedback, and editing have played a significant role in shaping this book, and I am truly grateful for their dedication and commitment to helping me realize my vision. Their generosity, kindness, and unwavering support have made all the difference, and I hope that this book will inspire others to pursue their dreams with passion and dedication.

This book stands as a testament to the incredible power of collaboration and the profound impact that can be achieved when individuals come together to share their knowledge, expertise, and experiences. Within this context, there are two special individuals whom I would like to name and acknowledge, as their contributions have been instrumental in shaping the outcome of this book.

First, I would like to express my thanks to **Sukanya Ghosh**, an old colleague and dear friend. Throughout the initial phase of the book, Sukanya has been my sounding board, lending her ears and insights to the development of the book's idea and various other matters. Despite the numerous phone calls and multiple drafts, I bombarded her with, she generously dedicated her time and provided invaluable feedback, helping to shape the book's content and ensuring that it truly reflects my voice. I am immensely grateful for her support and guidance, which have played a crucial role in making this book authentically mine.

The second individual I would like to acknowledge is **Subhamoy Das**. Like a character from a Bollywood film, Subhamoy entered the picture just before the interval, and stood there till the climax impacting book's shape, tone, structure, content, and overall outlook has been nothing short of transformative. While Subhamoy is a great friend, he has also taken on the role of a mentor throughout this journey. I cannot thank him enough for pushing me to think bigger and to give my absolute best, ensuring that the book resonates with readers and is worth their time. Countless hours were spent engaging in thought-provoking brainstorming sessions over the phone, and his guidance has been invaluable.

The acknowledgment section will not get complete without mention of **Sumeet Khullar**, a constant supporter, and dear friend, as well as the group **Boots and Crampons**, whose leadership and expertise created an unforgettable experience. Their collective presence has played an essential part in shaping the narrative of this book and has left an enduring impact on my personal and professional journey.

Thank you to all who have contributed to making this book possible, and I hope that readers will find it to be a valuable resource on their own journeys of self-discovery and growth.

Empty Your Bags. Unlock Your Potential.

About the Author

Ajay Rawat

Ajay Rawat, based in New Delhi, India, is a person with many talents. With a diverse skill set that includes writing, poetry, painting, illustration, photography, and creative direction, he has made a name for himself as a versatile and imaginative artist.

Ajay has an unparalleled interest in human behavior and is always ready to support those around him. His 13 years of international coaching have allowed him to further refine and sharpen his abilities.

Ajay has worked with a wide range of people as a volunteer, including teachers, doctors, students, and professionals. He has helped people overcome limiting beliefs and bring out their best.

Ajay is attempting to assist people in discovering joy and contentment in their lives in order to form a better world.

www.ingramcontent.com/pod-product-compliance
Lightning Source LLC
LaVergne TN
LVHW091530070526
838199LV00001B/1